Mr. Moonbeam and the Halloween Crystal

Moonbeam Children's Book Award for Pre-Teen Fiction, Ebook (Bronze), 2019

Readers' Favorite Book Award Winner for Holiday Fiction (Bronze), 2020

Purple Dragonfly Book Award Winner for Holiday Fiction (Second Place), 2021

FOR THE NORTHERN STAR PUBLISHING

Copyright © 2019 Ryan Cowan
Illustrations copyright © 2020 Halo Rife

All rights reserved. No part of this publication may be reproduced without written permission from the publisher.

ISBN: 9781097952779 (paperback)
ISBN: 9798351181905 (hardcover)

Book cover and interior design by David Miles

MR. MOONBEAM AND THE HALLOWEEN CRYSTAL

RYAN COWAN

ILLUSTRATIONS BY HALO RIFE, AGE 15

CONTENTS

Acknowledgments... 9

1 *Mr. Moonbeam*.. 11

2 *Mr. Moonbeam's Visit*................................... 19

3 *Cloak and Dagger!*.. 29

4 *Toil and Trouble*.. 35

5 *A Discussion*.. 43

6 *Classroom Drama*... 51

7 *Mr. Moonbeam's Moonlight Lesson*............. 63

8 *Storm's Advice*... 73

9 *Mossy Mansion*... 83

10 *A Haunted Mansion*..................................... 95

11 *Halloween Is In the Air!*............................. 109

12 *Moonstone*... 115

13 *Noir*.. 121

14 *Ginny Butler's Diary*.................................. 129

15 *A Conflict among Friends*......................... 137

16 *The Power of Invisibility*............................*141*
17 *The Fight Begins*.......................................*149*
18 *Elliott's Vision*..*157*
19 *Mr. Moonbeam's Resolve* *165*
20 *A Bargain*...*173*
21 *A Ghostly Plan*...*177*
22 *Truth See'er*..*185*
23 *A Town Meeting* *191*
24 *A Secret Weapon* *201*
25 *The Battle Begins*......................................*207*
26 *Separation* *217*
27 *The Dark Diamond of Disappearance*.............*223*
28 *The Witching Hour*...................................*227*
29 *Halloween*..*237*
30 *May It Be* *243*
31 *One More Time*..*249*
About the Author & Illustrator *252*

DEDICATION

*To Marybeth Mitchell,
Dodie Cleland,
and Larry Merrill*

ACKNOWLEDGMENTS

Just like Sloan Moonbeam, all around the world there are thousands of hard-working, dedicated, professional teachers making a difference in the lives of children every day. As a teacher myself, I would like to acknowledge all of my colleagues for their hard-work and dedication to the teaching profession. This book is about a teacher who relentlessly serves others with help from one special student along the way. Enjoy!

And a special thank you to Halo and David for taking this journey with me.

—RYAN

Mr. Moonbeam, Elliott, and Sabrina

1

MR. MOONBEAM

ELLIOTT WATCHED AS THE WIND AND rain came crashing down against his classroom window. The veins of whiteness that illuminated the dark sky fascinated him. The lightning flashes made him wince. He was thankful to be inside.

Another gray October day, he watched his third-grade teacher demonstrate the correct way to form a cursive "J." Squirming in his chair, he tried to get comfortable, but the wooden chair was so uncomfortable. His friend Lucas watched Elliott struggle to get comfortable. He watched Elliott grow frustrated with his writing.

Elliott was unhappy with his cursive "J." His loops looked too skinny. His slant looked too slanted. Mr.

Moonbeam could always make cursive handwriting look like the easiest thing in the world. Mr. Moonbeam was Elliott's teacher. He was a special teacher: Mr. Moonbeam had magical powers. The students in the class didn't know, but Elliott did.

Elliott watched Mr. Moonbeam write perfect letters on the board. Usually, Mr. Moonbeam's graceful movements made Elliott want to write. Today, the sound of the chalk—tap, click, scratch, tap, click, scratch—seemed to hypnotize Elliott. That and the sounds of the storm distracted Elliott from his work. His mind wandered to the Halloween decorations found throughout his classroom.

All around Elliott's classroom, the spirit and joy of Halloween was displayed and celebrated through colorful decorations. A wobbly pair of skeletons hung on the classroom door. A purple witch floated above the blackboard. He turned around to see the fiery skulls that stared back at him from the classroom windows. Their orange flames looked sinister and vibrant against the darkness of the storm. He could almost hear their spooky laughs. But it was the haunting orange jack-o-lanterns hanging on the closets that captivated Elliott's attention the most. In his mind, they floated off the wooden closets and hovered over the classroom, suspended in mid-air. Their eerie orange faces stared back at him. It seemed, for a minute, that Elliott was not in this world. It was as if he had been magically transported into some Halloween universe, when in reality, he was supposed to be practicing his cursive "J."

Indeed, the jack-o-lanterns, skeletons, witches, and skulls were spooky, and the raging storm outside made them even spookier. But Elliott was not afraid. He smiled because he loved his teacher, and he loved his teacher's Halloween decorations.

Elliott also loved Mr. Moonbeam's creativity, his sense of humor, and his quiet kindness. Mr. Moonbeam never lost his temper—even when students like Elliott failed to pay attention. He would simply say, "Pay attention, class." And the class would respond, "Yes, Mr. Moonbeam." Elliott loved this quiet, predictable routine.

"Okay, Elliott, concentrate!" he thought to himself.

Elliott managed to focus his attention back to the lesson when a flurry of thoughts distracted him again. Sometimes the children would have rainy day recess in their classroom and at other times it would be in the auditorium. With only a few minutes left until recess, the other students were silently wondering whether or not their rainy-day recess would be in the classroom or in the auditorium. The auditorium was better because they would all get to play basketball together. While Elliott's classmates silently thought about their recess, Elliott knew the answer already. For some reason, he always managed to just "know" certain things.

"It will be in the auditorium," he blurted out.

All of the students laughed, and Elliott felt embarrassed.

It wasn't Elliott's fault that he couldn't control his mouth. Sometimes these uncontrollable things just happened to him.

Mr. Moonbeam had clever techniques for quieting even the most disrespectful class. He gave a hand-signal which meant line up one by one, and the students lined up for rainy day recess. However, Elliott remained in his seat with his head down.

"Walk quietly to the auditorium. I will be there in a minute," Mr. Moonbeam said to his students.

"Yes, Mr. Moonbeam," they replied in unison.

After the students left, Mr. Moonbeam walked over to Elliott.

Elliott said, "I don't know what to do Mr. Moonbeam. It just happens. I can't control it." He raised his head and looked at his young teacher. Mr. Moonbeam had bright blue eyes, wavy brown hair, and pale, white skin.

Mr. Moonbeam sat down beside Elliott and said, "Try to remember Elliott, we were asked to live and interact with non-magical people for a reason. It's a huge responsibility. We must hide our powers as much as possible. That IS the rule. You are still developing your powers and your sensitivities are extremely sensitive. I'm starting to wonder.... Can you read minds?"

A surprised look came over Elliott's face. He looked at his teacher and said, "I don't know."

Mr. Moonbeam thought silently in his head and asked, "Can you read my mind, Elliott?"

They sat there for a moment while Elliott concentrated. He could hear the thunder outside. The flashes of lightning brightened the classroom in intervals.

He looked at Mr. Moonbeam but nothing came to mind. He looked at Mr. Moonbeam's glasses. In the lens he saw a white reflection that moved like a grayish cloud. The gray reflection distracted Elliott, and he was unable to read Mr. Moonbeam's mind.

"See! I can't do it when I want! It only happens when I don't want it to happen. Then, I do something like yell out loud or say something crazy," Elliott said. He was irritated.

"I don't think you've ever said anything crazy, Elliott," Mr. Moonbeam ruffled Elliott's hair. There was another crash of thunder as Elliott and his teacher shifted their gaze towards the window and the storm.

Once again, Elliott felt as if the fiery skulls on the classroom windows were staring at him.

"Tonight, I'm coming to your house for a meeting, and I'll be able to talk to your parents about all of this," Mr. Moonbeam said.

"Lucas is in the hall," Elliott said without looking.

Sure enough, Elliott's best friend Lucas was standing in the doorway.

"Can Elliott come to recess?" Lucas asked. "We are playing games in the auditorium and I . . . I . . . need a partner."

Mr. Moonbeam smiled, "Yes, Lucas! Elliott's not in trouble. Both of you are free to go to recess."

Mr. Moonbeam watched the boys walk down the hallway. Then, he walked over to the classroom window and looked at the storm. He thought about his math lesson. Did it work? Did the kids understand fractions? He wasn't sure. He thought about the mountain of papers that he had to grade and wished that there was a spell for grading papers. He thought about Elliott's giftedness and sensibilities and how Elliott was different from the others.

How was he going to teach this young sorcerer to focus on his school work and control his magic?

Then, he thought about something worse—something much bigger than the typical problems of a teacher—Halloween was quickly approaching.

As Elliott's teacher, Mr. Moonbeam had a lot of problems to solve, and he was not sure exactly how to do it. He watched as streaks of lightning illuminated the orange, fiery, paper skulls on the window in front of him . . .

2

MR. MOONBEAM'S VISIT

ELLIOTT'S PARENTS, GRETA AND Christian Keene, are powerful witches. Harnessing magical energy from nature and crystals, Greta can change into other forms. She is also an excellent crystal gazer which allows her to use crystals to seek answers to unknown questions. Her husband, Christian, uses Star Power to cast spells through daggers, and his magical cape protects him from powerful spells. Like all witches from Moonstone, Elliott's parents fly on magical brooms.

Magic did not come easily to Elliott. At times, his magic was unpredictable and uncontrollable. This bothered him even more than his messy room which happened to be littered with books, shoes, clothes, and toys. Elliott closed his eyes and listened to the music being played by the bewitched record player that his parents had brought from Moonstone. In his mind, he visualized the books, shoes, clothes, and toys moving by themselves.

The music helped him concentrate and one by one the books slowly rose, spun around, and found their way to the bookshelves. Several pairs of socks walked over and jumped into the hamper. His tennis shoes walked themselves to their place under the bed while several jackets, shirts, and pants floated to the closet and hung themselves neatly on hangers. He was pleased.

The music stopped and the needle on the enchanted record player moved back in place. "Now, for my toys," he mumbled.

Elliott breathed deeply and closed his eyes. In his mind, he visualized his stuffed animals placed neatly above his pillows. Then, he imagined his toy cars, his action figures, and his games placed on the shelf. Finally, he imagined his bedroom floor cleared completely. Then, he opened his eyes.

"Man!" Elliott said. To his disappointment, he was unable to use magic to move his stuffed animals, toys, and games as easily as he had moved his clothes and books.

"I wonder what went wrong?" he asked himself as he picked up the remainder of his mess.

Downstairs, Elliott's parents used their own magical powers to clean. An enchanted mop mopped the floor. A beautiful feather duster dusted and a vacuum cleaner vacuumed. Sparkly sponges washed dishes while bewitched towels dried and placed the dishes neatly in the cabinet.

Elliott's parents orchestrated these magical events beautifully, and as he walked downstairs, Elliott stopped and said, "Wow! This is cleaning!"

Elliott wanted to help his parents. They were busy and did not see their son standing at the bottom of the stairs. He stared intently at a broom by the closet and mumbled to himself:

A dusty floor
A messy room
Sweep the porch
Magical broom!

Suddenly, the door opened and Mr. Moonbeam was standing on the front porch. The bewitched broom zoomed out of the house and immediately began sweeping the porch. Mr. Moonbeam stared at the broom. The broom, which was suspended in mid-air, stopped sweeping and seemed to stare at Mr. Moonbeam.

"Oh no," Elliott thought while looking at his teacher and the enchanted broom.

Mr. Moonbeam and the broom stared at each other for a few seconds. Whenever Mr. Moonbeam moved left, the broom moved left. Whenever Mr. Moonbeam moved right, the broom moved right. He was cornered. Trapped!

Like a snake ready to strike, the broom inched closer and hit Mr. Moonbeam on the head. It smacked him from behind! Mr. Moonbeam moved, but no matter what, he could not shake the magical broom.

"Elliott! What have you done?" his mother gasped.

But, Elliott did not answer. He watched as his dad took out his sparkly wand and said:

"Be gone!"

And, with a quick wave, Elliott's dad flicked his wand and the broom flew back into the house—into the closet.

Elliott's dad walked towards Mr. Moonbeam and said, "Sloan, I'm very sorry."

Elliott thought that it was weird to hear his teacher called by his first name. His family and Sloan Moonbeam were the only witches who lived in the non-magical town called Wolf's End, so Mr. Moonbeam visited Elliott's parents often. They were good friends.

"It's okay, Christian. I have an idea whose magic this is?" With bright eyes, Mr. Moonbeam looked at Elliott.

"I was only trying to help." Elliott said sullenly.

"It's okay, Elliott. I know," Mr. Moonbeam said.

"Elliott's powers are so unpredictable, Sloan. Greta and I aren't sure what to do about it," Christian said.

Elliott's mom knelt down beside Elliott. She said, "You're going to be a great sorcerer someday, Elliott. Mr. Moonbeam is an excellent teacher!"

Mr. Moonbeam smiled, "Don't worry, Elliott. I'm going to help you develop your magic, but it is going take time, patience, and a plan. I'm always thinking about it."

Elliott felt better knowing that Mr. Moonbeam was working on a plan for his magic. He sat on the couch and admired his teacher's appearance.

Mr. Moonbeam wore black pants, a white buttoned shirt, a black vest, and a black velvet cloak. Wearing white gloves on both hands, Mr. Moonbeam placed his wand inside his cloak and removed his black top hat. Elliott wanted to grow up to be just like Mr. Moonbeam.

Mr. Moonbeam stood in the open doorway. Outside, the autumn breeze rattled the shutters of the house and sent orange, red, yellow, and gold leaves swirling through the air.

"Did you bring it?" Christian asked.

"The cauldron is ready," Greta said.

With glowing eyes, Mr. Moonbeam reached inside his cloak. He pulled out a medium-sized black box covered with moons and stars. He held the box in his gloved hand and walked into the house. The door closed by itself.

Elliott's eyes grew wider as he watched Mr. Moonbeam open the box to reveal a beautiful, shiny crystal ball which created reflections that danced on the walls of the dimly lit room.

"The Halloween Crystal," Mr. Moonbeam said.

"Ooh! Can I hold it, Mr. Moonbeam?" Elliott asked energetically.

"I'm afraid not, Elliott. This crystal is very delicate and incredibly powerful," Mr. Moonbeam said. Elliott felt disappointed.

A ball of crystallized snow, a miniature moon itself, the crystal glowed brightly. Elliott had never seen anything so beautiful. It lit up the entire room.

Christian turned towards his son and said, "Elliott, you have school tomorrow."

"Can I stay up and watch you summon, Enchantra?" Elliott asked.

"How did you know about Enchantra?" Elliott's mom asked.

"He was reading our minds." Mr. Moonbeam turned his face away from the crystal's glow and looked at Elliott's parents. Outside, the autumn winds blew against the house.

"Is this true, Elliott?" Greta asked as she looked at her son.

Elliott shrugged his shoulders and looked at Mr. Moonbeam. He had no idea what they were talking about. Reading minds? Elliott did not know what to say.

"Elliott is hearing thoughts. It is a psychic gift and that might be the beginning of something great!" Mr. Moonbeam smiled at Elliott and then turned his gaze back to the crystal.

"Yes, it is," Christian said. He put his arms around his son. His face was full of surprise.

Mr. Moonbeam closed the box and the shadowy reflections disappeared from the walls. "I had planned on talking to you about it tonight," he said.

"And we will," Elliott's dad looked serious. "But, now it is time for bed. Elliott, we will see you in the morning."

Elliott walked to the stairs and looked back. The three adults stood in front of the three glowing jack-o-lanterns. A warm fire burned in the fireplace. Inside the fireplace, a black cauldron bubbled sending steam up the chimney. Next to the fireplace, three magical magical brooms rested against the mantle. It was as if the brooms were listening to the conversation in the room.

Elliott said, "I read in one of my books that some witches say that Enchantra isn't really alive anymore. That she is a powerful goddess." Elliott looked concerned.

Mr. Moonbeam looked at Elliott, "Don't worry, Elliott. Enchantra is on our side. But you are right, she is VERY powerful."

Elliott walked up the stairs. He looked outside the small window midway up the stairs towards his room. The smell of the jack-o-lanterns and the blowing leaves made him excited for Halloween. He looked back at everyone and said, "Goodnight mom and dad. Goodnight Mr. Moonbeam."

"Goodnight," they all said together.

But, before continuing upstairs, Elliott ran back and hugged Mr. Moonbeam quickly. Then, he raced upstairs and got into bed.

3

CLOAK AND DAGGER!

"**E**LLIOTT LOVES YOU, SLOAN," GRETA said smiling.

Mr. Moonbeam said, "Having psychic abilities, well I don't need to tell you . . ."

He sat down on the dark, velvet sofa to drink tea with Elliott's parents who were both concerned and surprised to hear about Elliott's psychic gift. The fire that burned in the fireplace sent out rays of light that brightened the crystals and herbs scattered throughout the dimly lit living room. Mr. Moonbeam enjoyed the scent of pumpkin from the glowing jack-o-lanterns on the mantle of the fireplace.

Greta said, "Elliott's powers have always been unpredictable. Before you became his teacher, there were many times he lost control of his powers at school. It was second grade. Is that right, Christian? Yes. It was in second grade that he made all the books fly off the shelves in his classroom! Thank goodness Enchantra was able to reverse that instantly, so the teacher and the students would not remember that magical event. From that moment, I knew Elliott's powers were sensitive, but I never would have guessed Elliott to have psychic abilities. Are you sure? Could there be more to his abilities?"

Mr. Moonbeam explained to Elliott's parents, just as any good teacher would, that he had a strong suspicion that Elliott was hearing thoughts and that Elliott indeed had some degree of psychic abilities. However, it was too early to know exactly what Elliott was capable of doing, but that he would continue to monitor Elliott's developing powers.

After discussing Elliott, Greta stood up and waved her hand in a circle. In an instant, she was magically clothed in a black dress and a pointed hat. She sat down and centered her witchy hat over her long blonde hair and sipped her tea.

Christian walked over to the mirror that hung on

the wall. The others watched him say, "Cloak and dagger!" Like Greta, his clothes changed magically.

Indeed, it was quite a sight to see these three witches sitting in the living room drinking tea with the glowing jack-o-lanterns situated above the warm fire. Each one had their own distinct outfit. Greta wore a long black dress and a black pointed hat that was decorated with moons and stars. Her long blonde hair trailed down to her shoulders. Elliott looked more like his dad, Christian, who wore a dark suit with a purple vest and a large, shiny cloak. Hiding inside the cloak were several magical daggers that glowed.

Mr. Moonbeam himself looked like some old magician's ghost. Top hats were his favorite! And, he had a wide selection of top hats to choose from—usually choosing a different one for each occasion. Tonight, he wore a plain, dark top hat and of course his cape, suit, and vest. But it was his white gloves that made him look so shiny and magical. They seemed to glow as he sipped his tea and enjoyed the evening.

After a while Mr. Moonbeam said, "We can talk about Elliott later. The cauldron is ready and Syballine will be expecting us."

Syballine, another guardian chosen by Enchantra, had been allowed to stay in Moonstone.

Mr. Moonbeam reached into his pocket and pulled out a silver horse the size of a toad. "I brought, Storm. He will stay behind and watch Elliott."

He sat the miniature horse down on the floor, and the three witches stood back and watched as the horse grew bigger and bigger until it was almost normal "horse" size.

The horse said, "It was getting hot in there, Sloan."

Greta walked over to the horse. "Storm, will you keep an eye on Elliott? He's upstairs sleeping." She rubbed his nose.

"It would be an honor," the magical horse bowed down.

After that, the three witches walked outside to a full moon painted against a clear, starry sky. The crisp autumn air smelled fresh as Mr. Moonbeam looked up at the moon. His eyes glowed, and he became filled with moon magic—the source of his power.

Opening his cape, Christian looked to the stars and became enchanted also. His magical daggers glowed brightly through his cape.

Greta breathed deeply and clutched the small crystal that hung around her neck. The smell of the earth, the leaves on the trees, the wind and everything in nature worked to energize her.

A trail of sparkles followed their brooms as Mr. Moonbeam led the three witches over the small town of Wolf's End.

Greta looked down at the trees. Their autumn leaves swayed lightly in the breeze. Christian watched the river which looked like a black snake in the night as it traversed its way through the small town. Together they flew, through the lazy smoky ghosts, which rose from the chimneys, towards the dark autumn forest ahead.

4

TOIL AND TROUBLE

THEY LANDED GENTLY BESIDE A GLOWing cauldron, and a beautiful witch with white skin and dark hair stood behind the eerie purplish glow. Like Greta, she wore a dark dress and a witch's hat.

Night time in a pine forest is both peaceful and magical. As Mr. Moonbeam and the others hugged and exchanged greetings, a family of owls perched on a branch, looked down on the four witches. The owls' green eyes glowed from the fire that warmed the cauldron. The dark pine trees swayed.

Deep within the forest, families of deer, raccoons, skunks, and squirrels all stirred in their nests—suspicious of the witches that stood around the bubbling cauldron. But while the animals remained leery of the witches that had suddenly intruded on their peaceful sleep, Mr. Moonbeam and the others felt right at home as they looked up from their embraces to see a flock of fluttering bats fly towards the moon.

Syballine said, "Enchantra will be waiting. We must get started right away."

Christian added, "You're right. I feel an incredible sense of urgency this year."

Despite the urgency, Greta walked towards Syballine and said, "And your daughter. How is she?"

With no expression, Syballine looked at Mr. Moonbeam and said, "I was hoping to send her with you. She and the crystal are in terrible danger. Did you bring it?"

Mr. Moonbeam reached inside his cape and by magic pulled out the black box which was decorated with moons and stars. He opened it and everyone admired the shiny crystal ball as its glorious light illuminated the forests and the owls that watched overhead.

Syballine touched the glowing crystal and said, "It takes my breath away."

Mr. Moonbeam closed the box and the luminous pearl disappeared from sight. With glowing eyes, he stared deeply at Syballine. "Sabrina can stay with me. Send her as soon as possible."

"Thank you, Sloan," she lowered her head.

Grabbing the sides of her black dress, Syballine walked towards the bubbling cauldron which sent trails of steam, like ghosts, high above the trees. The others followed as the animals watched the four witches gather around the glowing cauldron.

The animals were the only non-magical living things able to witness the magic that was about to begin while the people of Wolf's End slept soundly in their beds.

"Everyone must join hands and form a circle," Syballine said extending her arms.

Syballine closed her eyes as they circled the cauldron and said, *"By ALL of our powers; the energy of the moon, the magic of the stars, the beauty of the Earth, and the darkness of night, I summon the great, Enchantra."*

The four witches watched as purple steam from the cauldron circled all around them. A swift wind carried the swirling mist up into the night sky and the forest animals stirred. During this magical moment, Mr. Moonbeam's eyes sparkled, Greta's crystal necklace turned bright red, and Christian's daggers glowed brightly through his cape. The owls in the trees fanned their wings.

Syballine looked up into the dissipating mist and said, *"Tell us what evil awaits this Halloween night!"*

Like little purple tornadoes, the misty steam that rose from the cauldron morphed into a series of colors: green, red, blue, and finally white. The white mist lingered for a minute and a face appeared magically.

The wise face in the steam stared at them and said, "Your daughter is in great danger, Syballine. Noir wants to kidnap her and steal the Halloween Crystal."

Enchantra turned slowly towards Mr. Moonbeam and said, "Show me the crystal."

Once again, Mr. Moonbeam reached inside his cape and opened the box. Enchantra's misty hand reached for the glowing crystal, "It is a wonder, a magical wonder. Only the purest heart should ever touch it." She looked intently at Mr. Moonbeam who felt uncomfortable under her witchy stare.

"It is incredibly powerful," Mr. Moonbeam said as he closed the box. The bright light faded as he tried to hide his nervousness.

Enchantra looked at all of them and breathed deeply. Her voice became stronger. Her face became harder. "The veil between the two worlds is paper thin on Halloween—AND—NOIR—KNOWS—THIS! With the crystal, he would be able to overcome even the most powerful spell and enter this world on Halloween. Monsters, vampires, demons, hags, and werewolves are just a few of the creatures he would bring into this world. They would spread REAL evil and terror on Halloween night. But even worse, the crystal's power would allow Noir to rule over all of Moonstone. Our beautiful world would succumb to his dark forces and all would be lost as he would be the all-powerful ruler of both worlds."

The four witches stared at the cauldron. They stared at Enchantra's face in the steam and felt her powerful presence. Even the forest animals hid from her booming voice and the seriousness of the situation. Mr. Moonbeam looked up and noticed that the owls who had been watching them so intently were suddenly gone.

Enchantra turned towards Syballine and said, "Noir will try to take Sabrina from you. Her powers are great, still developing, but great. And, she is easily persuaded by material things. But, you know this already." Enchantra looked concerned.

Syballine stood proudly, "Yes, I know."

Enchantra looked at Syballine for a moment and paused. Mr. Moonbeam felt uncomfortable as she shifted her gaze to him and said, "As the guardians of this world, you must stop Noir. You all know that non-magical people must never learn of our magical world. It is forbidden. As guardians, you must protect non-magical people and our secret world. It would be best to hide the crystal. Do whatever it takes to make sure dark magic does not enter this world on Halloween night. There is another who can help."

Greta asked, "Who?"

Enchantra looked at Greta, "I will not say, but you will be surprised."

Enchantra said, "Noir's powers are great. I am counting on the four of you to keep the crystal safe, protect Moonstone, protect the non-magical world and keep our magical existence a secret."

Syballine spoke up, "Isn't that a lot to ask of us?"

Enchantra turned and stared at her for a moment, "Yes . . . yes it is. I acknowledge that. But, you were all chosen for a reason."

Syballine responded, "But is that enough? Will we receive any help at all?"

Mr. Moonbeam moved beside Syballine.

Enchantra looked at both of them and said, "Non-magical people must never learn of our magical ways. It is written in the Witches' Code of Conduct. Sloan Moonbeam will lead you."

Mr. Moonbeam's heart skipped a beat. He felt the weight of the world on his shoulders.

Enchantra finished by saying, "I hope you will be able to save Halloween, protect Syballine's daughter, and realize your own magical destinies. It will be a struggle."

Enchantra looked at Mr. Moonbeam and disappeared. Only the white mist from the cauldron remained as the wind blew through the trees.

5

A DISCUSSION

After Enchantra's magical exit, the four witches flew back to Elliott's house for a discussion.

Syballine was the first to speak. "I will send Sabrina tomorrow. It is too dangerous for her to stay in Moonstone. I realize now that Noir will stop at nothing to kidnap her. At least, I know she'll be safe here until Halloween. I feel better leaving her with you, Sloan."

Once again, Mr. Moonbeam felt a tremendous amount of responsibility. Clearly, Enchantra had made him the leader in this fight, and he wasn't sure whether he wanted that position or responsibility.

Despite his doubts, Mr. Moonbeam said, "Elliott will be there to help her adjust to the other students in the class."

Greta looked at Mr. Moonbeam, "Yes, although, that will be a lot of unpredictable magic in one classroom. Are you sure you can keep their powers a secret from the non-magical students?"

He said, "I'll do my best."

Christian placed his hand on Mr. Moonbeam's shoulder. "I can't think of a better teacher. It seems like yesterday that we were all students"

Greta said, "Yes, it went by too fast. And, I miss Moonstone terribly. Living in this non-magical world is not easy, but we all do our best. Sloan has the hardest job—being a teacher. I know it is hard for you to hide your true identity from your students and parents."

"It is hard, but we are all here to protect this world. I'm focused on my purpose. Noir only wants the crystal's power, and he would do anything to get it. He has no problem breaking the most sacred rule in the Witches' Code of Conduct," Mr. Moonbeam said.

The four witches sat in the living room by the fire. the Witches' Code of Conduct was a set of rules and expectations written down for all the witches, sorcerers, wizards and magical beings of Moonstone. The

A DISCUSSION

code prohibited such things as telling non-magical people about magic, using magic on non-magical people, and entering into marriage with a non-magical person. There are many rules and policies written in Moonstone's Witches' Code of Conduct.

Christian replied, "You mean the code that prohibits using magic on non-magical people?"

Mr. Moonbeam nodded and said, "Enchantra and the council have placed limits on Noir's magic, but it is a struggle to keep those limits in place. There will always be resistance."

Syballine sipped her tea and spoke, "Enchantra said to hide the Halloween Crystal from Noir. I wonder what she meant by that? And, I also wonder who is this "other" person that can help?"

Mr. Moonbeam said, "I'm not sure. Even without the crystal, Noir's powers could allow him to cross over into this world in a disguised form. He could be here right now looking for the crystal. The spell cast by Enchantra and the council was a powerful spell. It severely limited Noir's powers in this world. Even so, he could be here right now looking for the crystal in a form we do not recognize."

For many years, Noir the dark sorcerer has been feared throughout Moonstone. As the ruler of the Dark

Lands, he is the most powerful villain in Moonstone. Noir's gigantic, gothic castle sits high on the mountains overlooking the Dark Lands. He controls the vampires, werewolves, and evil hags that live throughout his kingdom.

Syballine said, "We are all "disguised" in this world!"

Mr. Moonbeam added, "Exactly! The crystal would give him the power to enter this world physically, and I have no doubt that he, or someone else, is watching this world, RIGHT NOW. It is certain! Noir knows the crystal isn't in Moonstone."

Christian took a silver dagger out of his cloak and held it up. "If that is true, Sloan, then, you are in terrible danger because you always have the crystal with you. We must think of a hiding place quickly."

Greta spoke, "Syballine could take the crystal back to Moonstone. That would put Noir on a wild goose chase!"

Syballine said, "That is too risky. Noir's lackeys are continually searching Moonstone for the crystal."

Syballine knew that at this very moment Noir's vampires and monsters were traveling all over Moonstone looking for the Halloween Crystal. They entered the homes of villagers and stormed the castles of the council members who had imposed limits on Noir's magic.

A DISCUSSION

Syballine continued, "No, it is better to hide it here. Everyone in Moonstone is terrified of Noir. They are counting on us to hide the crystal and keep it safe in this world. After all, Noir can't enter this world. That makes it harder for him."

Greta walked over to the fireplace and admired the flames. She thought for a moment and asked, "Can I see the crystal?"

Mr. Moonbeam reached into his cloak and handed Greta the black box with its moons and stars. She opened the box and held the glowing wonder in her hand so that she could use her gazing powers to peer deep inside the crystal's glowing magic.

She saw autumn trees with golden leaves that swayed like fans. The crystal showed her the non-magical town, Wolf's End, and the winding river that ran through it.

Then, the image passed swiftly over the trees and dove into the river. She saw the river's bottom clearly and the plants that swayed in the current. Suddenly, the image came out of the water to show an old vine covered mansion that stood on a hill. After that, the image vanished. The vision was so intense that Greta gasped and almost dropped the box.

"We should hide the crystal in the river," Greta said breathlessly.

Syballine stood up and said, "Is that what you saw?"

Greta said, "Well first, I saw the trees and the river that runs through town. Then, the vision dove down to the river's bottom and the vision changed to an image of an old house. I've never seen the house before. It was covered in moss."

They all looked at each other.

Syballine said, "What if we lose the crystal in the water?"

Greta answered, "There's an underwater cave in the river. I've been there before."

Mr. Moonbeam asked, "You saw a house in the vision?"

"An old mansion . . . I think . . . by the river," Greta said.

Christian spoke up, "There isn't an old mansion by the river, but there is an abandoned house on Rose Hill."

Syballine said, "I suggest we hide the crystal first and worry about the house later."

Greta agreed by saying, "Christian and I can hide the crystal first thing tomorrow."

"And, I'll check out the house," Mr. Moonbeam said.

After everything was settled, Mr. Moonbeam stood on the front porch and watched Syballine head for

A DISCUSSION

Moonstone on her broom. After she left, he climbed onto his broom and flew towards his non-magical home. Greta and Christian slept.

Elliott, however, was not asleep. While gazing out his window, his mind unexpectedly picked up the thoughts of his parents, his teacher, and Syballine. He watched Mr. Moonbeam fly towards the moon. He smiled at the trail of sparkles that fell like silver glitter from his teacher's broom. He knew every detail of their discussion, and he wanted to help. After thinking it over he tried to sleep, but it was hard because the moon was so bright. From his bedroom window, he watched as Mr. Moonbeam's glittery sparkles died one by one. He finally fell asleep.

In his dreams, he imagined Noir, the dark sorcerer riding one of his red and black dragons across the magical countryside that stretched throughout Moonstone. Elliott had never been to the magical world where his parents and Mr. Moonbeam were from. In his dream, he saw the cottages and villages which were scattered throughout Moonstone. He also saw Noir's monsters breaking into homes—looking for the Halloween Crystal. The sight of an old, haggard witch with green skin flashed in his dream, and he woke up suddenly. The images of Noir, his dragons, the vampires, and the witch caused his heart to beat rapidly. He ran to the window to look outside but nothing was there. Elliott had realized that Noir and his evil monsters were constantly looking for the Halloween Crystal. He wanted his parents to hide it soon!

The next day, Elliott's parents headed towards the river to hide the crystal. It was easy for Greta. She simply changed herself into a mermaid, swam to the river's bottom, and hid the crystal in an underwater cave. Elliott saw this in his mind and felt better.

6

CLASSROOM DRAMA

"WE HAVE A NEW STUDENT TODAY. Her name is, Sabrina," Mr. Moonbeam said as he introduced Sabrina to the class.

Sabrina stood timidly in front of the students. Except for her long red hair, she looked like a miniature version of her mother. She missed her castle and Moonstone. Would she be able to control her magic? Would the other kids like her? She knew that she could not perform any magic around non-magical people. However, she was used to using magic for everything. Elliott smiled at her. She smiled back and took her seat.

A student named Allison raised her hand and said, "Mr. Moonbeam. What group will Sabrina be in?"

Mr. Moonbeam thought about it, "Well, I'm not sure right now, Allison. I'll need to wait a little before I make that decision." Dressed in a clean, pressed black shirt, gray pants, and a gray tie, Mr. Moonbeam was a color-coordinated professional.

"Well, it would be all right with me if you put her in my group," Allison said as she smiled at Sabrina.

Elliott leaned over to Sabrina, "You don't want to be in HER group. She is the biggest KNOW IT ALL you can imagine."

Allison gave Elliott a mean look, but Elliott didn't pay any attention to it.

Mr. Moonbeam adjusted his glasses and raised his voice slightly, "Let's not talk about groups right now. As I told you on Friday, today you will have a short test over your multiplication facts. So, take out a pencil and a piece of paper to use as a cover sheet."

Elliott raised his hand.

"Yes," Mr. Moonbeam said.

"I just wanted to pass out the tests. I knew you wanted a paper passer," Elliott said.

Mr. Moonbeam could tell it was going to be one of those days. All the students were a little restless because of the new student.

Mr. Moonbeam let Elliott pass out the tests. The room became quiet, and he sat down to grade the stack of papers on his desk.

After a few minutes, Allison yelled, "Mr. Moonbeam! Mr. Moonbeam!"

"Allison! You need to be quiet! This is a test!" Mr. Moonbeam exclaimed.

"It's just that, well, Sabrina has playing cards in her desk, and you know the rules about bringing cards to school." Allison stared at Sabrina and made a half-smile.

Mr. Moonbeam sighed, "Do you have cards in your desk, Sabrina?"

Sabrina replied, "Yes, I have my Tarot Cards."

Allison interrupted, "What are Tarot Cards?"

Mr. Moonbeam got up quickly. "It doesn't matter Allison. Sabrina will give them to me, and you will take your test quietly."

Mr. Moonbeam held out his hand, and Sabrina quietly gave him the Tarot Cards. Elliott watched Allison. He did not like the way that she was treating Sabrina.

Mr. Moonbeam looked at Sabrina with urgency. "You know you're not allowed to bring materials *LIKE THIS* to school," he said secretly.

"Yes, Sloan—I mean Mr. Moonbeam—I'm sorry." Sabrina awkwardly picked up her pencil and took her test.

Meanwhile, Elliott became angry. He started to feel uncomfortable, like something bad was going to happen. "Mr. Moonbeam, Mr. Moonbeam! May I go to the restroom?" he asked.

"Is it an emergency? You are taking a test, Elliott," Mr. Moonbeam said sternly.

"Yes, it is a MAJOR emergency!" Elliott said jumping up and down. He couldn't sit still. As his anger grew, he became worried that he might lose control of his magic in front of the non-magical students.

"Go ahead," Mr. Moonbeam sighed.

Mr. Moonbeam slouched down in his chair and took a deep breath. His students were not focused on their work. Perhaps it was too soon for Sabrina to participate in a normal school setting. He recognized that she was having a difficult time adjusting to life in the non-magical world.

While Mr. Moonbeam thought about Sabrina, Elliott got up to go to the restroom. On his way out, a book from his desk hurled itself across the room and hit Allison on the back of her head.

"Ouch! Hey! Who threw that?" Allison said while

turning her head around. Allison saw Sabrina chuckle.

"Mr. Moonbeam! Mr. Moonbeam! Sabrina threw a book at me!" Allison exclaimed. Sabrina looked surprised. All the students turned their heads simultaneously towards Allison.

"Non-magical people are weird," Sabrina thought. "In Moonstone, a kid would have never behaved like such a cry-baby in front of their peers." She looked at the Halloween decorations in the classroom.

Lucas spoke up, "Sabrina didn't throw a book at you. I did!" All eyes turned from Allison to Lucas.

Sabrina stopped looking at the Halloween decorations and thought, "Who is this kid named, Lucas?"

Mr. Moonbeam looked at Lucas with disbelief and said, "Lucas, did you really throw a book at Allison?" All of the students looked at Mr. Moonbeam.

For a minute, Lucas hesitated. Then he said, "No, but I would like to. Anyway, I know that Sabrina didn't throw the book. It came from somewhere over there." All the students in the class turned their heads simultaneously towards Elliott's desk.

While the students were distracted, Mr. Moonbeam walked towards Allison's desk to pick up the book that had been thrown. When he saw the title, *Scary Tales of Witches, Warlocks, and Ghosts*, he quickly hid the book under his arm.

Mr. Moonbeam took a deep breath and walked to the front of the room. All eyes followed him as he said, "I can see that we are not going to get much work done this morning. Lucky for you, it is time for recess. I think we all need a break. Line up one by one." Mr. Moonbeam secretly pulled back his sleeve to look at his magical watch.

Elliott walked into the room, and Allison gave him a dirty look as she and the others lined up for recess. Mr. Moonbeam watched Elliott find his place in line and said, "Elliott and Sabrina, I want you to stay in for recess. The rest of you are dismissed."

The noisy students walked out of the room and ran towards the playground; however, Lucas stayed behind. Mr. Moonbeam knew that he was waiting for his number one friend, Elliott.

"Go on Lucas. Elliott will be out in a minute," Mr. Moonbeam said.

Reluctantly, Lucas left and followed the others to the yard. Then, Mr. Moonbeam motioned for Sabrina and Elliott to sit down. He sat down too.

"You lost control of your powers, didn't you?" Mr. Moonbeam asked as he looked intently at Elliott.

"Yes, but I did the right thing. I left the room. It's not my fault that the book flew across the room before I left," Elliott pleaded.

Sabrina looked at Elliott. "Thanks Elliott. But I can take care of myself." She was annoyed with this whole non-magical situation. It seemed petty and stupid to her.

Mr. Moonbeam looked at both of them. "We are ALL going to have to take care of each other. Nobody said this was going to be easy. You both have to control your magic around non-magical people. It is ABSOLUTELY against the rules to use magic on or around non-magical people. Remember, we are here to protect these people—not harm them. And, believe it or not, we need them as much as they need us. You are both going to have to behave appropriately at all times. It is a great responsibility." Mr. Moonbeam's tone was serious.

Sabrina said, "You have to admit, Mr. Moonbeam. She is ANNOYING!"

"Yeah, and she doesn't like Sabrina," Elliott said.

"How do you know?" Sabrina asked feeling slightly more engaged in the petty situation.

"I read her mind. She thinks you are too pretty," Elliott said. "And, she's jealous."

"Too pretty!" Sabrina smiled. "And, she's jealous?" she asked.

Elliott rolled his eyes.

Mr. Moonbeam interjected, "Excuse me . . . she is my student just like the two of you. Elliott, is it right for you to go around telling the personal thoughts of others? How would you like it if someone told your personal thoughts and secrets?"

Elliott thought for a moment, but he did not answer. He wanted to go outside and play with Lucas.

Sabrina added, "I don't see what is so great about this world. There's no magic, no castles, and no enchanted forests or animals. The people are rude, and the food is horrible! I miss my enchanted herb garden." Sabrina lowered her head.

Mr. Moonbeam raised Sabrina's chin gently. He felt sorry for her. "I know you miss your magical life, but you will learn a great deal from this experience. You will learn how to control your magic and live by your wits and intuition instead of living mainly by magic. Living here will sharpen your senses, broaden your mind to new ideas, and require you to accept that some things in life do not come easily." Mr. Moonbeam thought he was finally getting through to the children.

"But, I've always gotten everything I've ever wanted," Sabrina admitted. Elliott rolled his eyes again. He wasn't sure if he liked Sabrina or not.

"I guess I'm not getting through to them," Mr. Moonbeam thought.

"Your mother is worried about you too. That's another reason why she sent you here," Sabrina looked away while Mr. Moonbeam talked.

"While you're here, you are my responsibility, so I need you to cooperate and learn from this experience. And, please try to get along with Elliott. There is a great deal of danger involved as well. Noir wants to KIDNAP you and take the crystal," Mr. Moonbeam added.

"Wow," Elliott said wide-eyed.

Sabrina's face became serious. She said, "Noir wants revenge against my mother, and that's why he wants to kidnap me."

Mr. Moonbeam said, "It is more complicated than that. It's a long story that goes back to the Great Magical Civil War of Moonstone. You are safer in this world because Noir cannot physically enter this world. However, he may find an alternate way to enter this world, like a disguise, so we must be careful." He did not want to upset Sabrina.

Elliott asked, "But if Noir is disguised, doesn't that make him more dangerous?"

Mr. Moonbeam answered, "Yes and no, Elliott. By disguised, I mean, that he cannot interact with this world. He can only observe it in a disguised form. It is the result of a curse placed on him a long time ago by the Council of Witches and Enchantra. It helps protect non-magical people, and it means that this world is a safe haven for many witches—like Sabrina for instance. Now, do you see why we need these people too? Noir may be watching, but there is nothing he can do. However, with the Halloween Crystal, all of that would change. Noir would be able to do terrible things to this world and our own world, Moonstone. As a matter of fact, it was the crystal's power that allowed Enchantra and the others to place those magical restrictions on him." Mr. Moonbeam enjoyed the looks of curiosity that stared back at him. Now, he had them in the palm of his hand!

The children were quiet. Getting up from his desk, Mr. Moonbeam stood up and placed a gentle hand on their shoulders. "Now, after school, you will both accompany me to the old mansion on Rose Hill. Elliott, your mother saw a vision of that house in the Halloween Crystal. I feel this experience will give you a chance to practice your magic. You will both have that to look forward to for the rest of the day!" he said.

"Lucas is at the door," Elliott said.

Mr. Moonbeam turned around and said, "Lucas! You are supposed to be outside." He wondered how long the boy had been standing there.

"Can Elliott come out and play?" he asked.

Mr. Moonbeam said, "Yes, you may all go outside, but please stay out of trouble." He looked at Elliott and Sabrina with a serious face. They nodded.

The children walked outside, and Mr. Moonbeam stood by the window. He watched Elliott and Sabrina swing on the swings. It was a beautiful fall day.

Somehow, Mr. Moonbeam would have to keep the peace between these children while teaching and protecting them. He was nervous.

7

MR. MOONBEAM'S MOONLIGHT LESSON

MR. MOONBEAM WATCHED THE last student leave his class. School was out but he remained at school with Elliott and Sabrina for several hours. The two children played board games and colored Halloween pictures while Mr. Moonbeam graded papers.

Being in a school after hours is very different than being in school during the day. The hallways become silent. The playground is empty.

MR. MOONBEAM AND THE HALLOWEEN CRYSTAL

Despite this empty silence, you can still feel the energy of all the children that attended school throughout the day. Their voices and laughter seem to whisper down the hallways in the quiet hours before and after school.

Sloan Moonbeam's classroom was cozier than most elementary school classrooms. Any observer could tell that Mr. Moonbeam was not your standard, run-of-the-mill, teacher. His classroom environment was a cut above the rest with its meticulously arranged furniture, neat bookshelves, globes, maps, charts, and exceptional student work posted on every decorated bulletin board.

Situated below these bulletin boards were the class pets: an aquarium with a variety of tropical fish and plants, a beautiful goldfish bowl with several swimming goldfish, and a cage with two hamsters who at this very minute were busy running quickly on the wheel.

Mr. Moonbeam was a teacher who exemplified both neatness and studiousness. But, within his pursuit of perfection, Mr. Moonbeam also knew how to have fun with his students.

As Elliott and Sabrina played board games, Elliott looked up at the Halloween decorations which were so neatly displayed throughout the classroom and smiled. He loved being at school, especially after his classmates were gone.

When the sun finally set, Elliott and Sabrina watched their teacher use magic to change from a teacher into a sorcerer! They were amazed! He looked enchanting in his long black cape with its silver lining. His white shirt, gloves, and sparkly black vest lit up the dark classroom. To the children, he looked like the ghost of an old magician from centuries ago.

Mr. Moonbeam's eyes glowed as he walked towards the window. Taking deep breaths, he looked at the moon while the children watched him glow and change.

"What's he doing?" Elliott whispered to Sabrina who was busy putting away the games. He could tell by the look on her face that she was annoyed by his question.

"He's getting magic from the moon, silly. Don't you know anything about magic?" Sabrina's tone was arrogant.

Elliott felt embarrassed. He knew that he had a limited knowledge of magic and witchcraft, and he was annoyed by Sabrina's criticism and negative attitude.

"I was only asking," he said.

He hopped down from the desk and walked towards the window. Mr. Moonbeam stood in the moonlight as they both looked outside.

The gentle autumn winds shook the leaves from their trees. By moonlight, Elliott watched a single leaf drift slowly down from the branch of an old oak tree. The feathery leaf floated past the window and landed softly on the window sill.

The quiet, peaceful evening made Elliott think of a song he often played on his bewitched record player. He watched as the calm breeze made the swings on the playground sway back and forth as if some invisible ghost was pushing them gently.

"What are you thinking about?" Mr. Moonbeam asked.

Elliott turned towards his teacher, "I was just thinking about a song. I like music, and I was watching the swings move back and forth by themselves."

Mr. Moonbeam said, "Could be a ghost . . . "

Elliott wasn't sure if his teacher was serious or joking.

Sabrina walked towards them and snapped her fingers. A flame appeared on her fingertip. "I like fire! My mom says it is because of my red hair."

Sabrina's flame lit up the dark classroom creating shadows on the walls. This made Mr. Moonbeam's

MR. MOONBEAM'S MOONLIGHT LESSON

Halloween decorations even spookier—especially the paper jack-o-lanterns that stared back from the closet.

Mr. Moonbeam blew out Sabrina's flame.

"Hey," she said.

"Sorry kids, but no magic in class. You know the rules," Mr. Moonbeam smiled at the kids.

Sabrina said, "But you are using magic?"

"Yes, but I'm the teacher," Mr. Moonbeam smiled at Sabrina. He knew she was used to getting her way with everything.

"Mr. Moonbeam," Elliott asked. "Why is it that every witch has something that they like more than anything—something that adds to their powers?"

In the dark classroom, Mr. Moonbeam bent down to look at the children. The hamsters were busy running.

Mr. Moonbeam said, "That's a good question, Elliott. You see, every witch or warlock gets magical energy from some source. For example, my magical energy comes from the moon. Elliott, your mother gets her powers from nature and crystals while your father gets magic from the stars." Mr. Moonbeam pointed towards the billions of stars that sparkled outside.

Sabrina added, "All witches have some source of natural enchantment. My mom says my powers come from fire and the sun."

"I think she's right," Mr. Moonbeam said smiling. "Your mother gets her powers from *Night Magic*. *Night Magic* is very powerful, but it can only be used at night."

Sabrina said, "That's why my mom sleeps all day and stays awake all night. She's a night witch. And, Enchantra, my mom says that Enchantra is so powerful that she doesn't age. After 200 years, she still looks the same."

"What about me?" Elliott asked wide-eyed.

With glowing eyes, Mr. Moonbeam looked at Elliott, "You are kind of special Elliott. You have the ability to hear thoughts, read, and understand people. Your sensibilities are sincere, sensitive, and perceptive, but unfortunately, they are also highly unpredictable. I think your magical energy comes from something very special, but I'm not sure yet."

Sabrina smiled at Elliott while flames shot out of her eyes.

"Hey!" Elliott said.

"You didn't read that thought beforehand, *Mr. MINDREADER!*" she laughed.

Mr. Moonbeam smiled. "All right, this moonlight lesson is over. Now, we're off to Rose Hill and the abandoned house." Mr. Moonbeam walked over to feed the fish and turn off the light on the aquarium. The kids followed him.

MR. MOONBEAM'S MOONLIGHT LESSON

Sabrina asked, "Why are we going to a place called Rose Hill, Sloan?"

"Why do you call him, Sloan?" Elliott asked as he watched his teacher feed the fish.

"Because that is his name—dummy—and I can call him that if I want," Sabrina replied arrogantly.

Elliott looked at Mr. Moonbeam and asked, "Can I call you Sloan?"

Mr. Moonbeam waved his hand and silenced the children for a moment. They tried to talk but couldn't because he had them under a "silent spell."

Once he finished feeding the class pets, he turned around and said, "I want you both to call me, Mr. Moonbeam. Is that understood?" He tried to be serious with the kids. Once again, he was tickled by their innocence and inquisitiveness. His eyes continued to glow.

The children nodded in unison. Neither one of them had been silenced before.

A ray of moonlight shined mysteriously through the classroom window and fell on Mr. Moonbeam's face. In the moonlight, he looked different. He no longer looked like a teacher. He looked more like a sorcerer. Elliott watched the fish swim in the moonlight.

Mr. Moonbeam leaned over and spoke to the children in a spooky voice. Their eyes widened.

He said, "There is an evil sorcerer from Moonstone. His name is, Noir. He is dark, powerful, and very, very clever, but he wants more power. He wants the greatest power—the Halloween Crystal! If he succeeds in his plan, he will enter this world on Halloween night. But, he won't come alone. He will bring monsters, vampires, ghosts, disgusting hags, and werewolves with him! He will capture this world as well as Moonstone."

Mr. Moonbeam was a great storyteller. Not only did he change his voice, but he also used hand gestures to capture the children's attention.

He continued, "We were sent here to protect this world and use our magic for good. We must keep our magic a secret because that is how it is written in the Witches' Code of Conduct. Non-magical people can never know that witches exist. You will both learn a great deal from this experience." Mr. Moonbeam backed away from the children who looked startled. He had given them enough background knowledge. He had succeeded in sparking their interests.

He asked, "Do you understand?"

Sabrina and Elliott both nodded. In his mind, Elliott thought about the conversation Mr. Moonbeam had had earlier with his parents and Sabrina's mother. He knew where the Halloween Crystal was hidden. And,

MR. MOONBEAM'S MOONLIGHT LESSON

he knew all about Enchantra and the house on Rose Hill. However, he chose to keep this information a secret from Mr. Moonbeam and the others. In a small way, it bothered him that he was able to perceive the most secretive thoughts of others, but he didn't know how to admit that he knew this information.

Mr. Moonbeam snapped his fingers. The children breathed a sigh of relief that they were finally able to speak, but before Sabrina could open her mouth, Mr. Moonbeam quickly placed his finger over his lips.

"Not a word," he said. Wide-eyed, they both agreed to be silent.

Mr. Moonbeam took out his magic wand and waved it several times in a circle. The room seemed to spin and Elliott and Sabrina watched as vivid colors magically filled the dark room. Everything moved in circles, spinning with the colors, the Halloween decorations, the desks, the chairs . . . the classroom pets watched as real magic was actually happening. And in a an instant, they were transported from their dark classroom to the foot of a hill. Dead rose bushes lined a path that led up to an old moss-covered mansion covered in vines.

Under the full moon, Mr. Moonbeam looked at the children, "Now, we will explore this house and try to figure out why Elliott's mother saw it in the Halloween Crystal. Be alert, be prepared, and be quiet."

8

STORM'S ADVICE

THE DARK, CHILLY AUTUMN AIR CAUSED Elliott to shiver as he looked around. Just a few seconds ago, he had been inside his cozy classroom, but now he was standing at the base of a huge hill. He was surrounded by creepy looking trees covered in orange, red, yellow, and gold leaves. Elliott could smell the leaves as they crunched under his feet.

Elliott and Sabrina looked at the old mansion that stood tall at the top of the hill. High in the sky, the full moon shined brightly behind the old brown and gray house and Elliott watched as a group of bats flew from the chimney of the house towards the yellow moon.

The children walked towards their teacher, who was standing near a pile of dead leaves, and watched Mr. Moonbeam gaze at the yellow moon. His eyes started to glow as his enchanted powers grew from the moon's energy.

Then, Mr. Moonbeam reached inside his cloak and pulled out his wand again. Sparks flew from the tip of the wand as he waved it in the air and tapped the top of his head. The children smiled as a large black top hat appeared magically above their teacher's shiny hair. The moon's yellow rays made Mr. Moonbeam look magical.

Suddenly, Mr. Moonbeam spun around quickly and pointed his wand at the children and said:

> *By the moon*
> *And all its magic*
> *Tonight...*
> *Give these children*
> *The clothes, the hats, and the wands*
> *To make it right!*

In a magical instant, Elliott and Sabrina were transformed.

Sabrina twirled around slowly in the crunchy leaves and admired her velvety black dress and red-laced

STORM'S ADVICE

boots. Mr. Moonbeam had also given her a witchy red velvet hat. In her hand, she held a glowing red wand that was tipped with a bright purple star.

Elliott's outfit was just as magical as Sabrina's. Looking down, he admired his black pants and shirt, green vest and cape, and hat which was decorated with green stars. Mr. Moonbeam had given Elliott black boots and a black wand with a green tip that glowed. The children stared at each other in amazement. Mr. Moonbeam was pleased.

Mr. Moonbeam reached inside his cloak and pulled out his tiny, silver horse. He laid the miniature horse on the ground and stepped back. Sabrina and Elliott watched as the tiny horse grew before their eyes.

"Awesome!" they both said in unison.

Like Mr. Moonbeam, Storm glowed under the moonlight. He bowed and in a deep voice said, "Good evening."

"Storm, I want you to meet Syballine's daughter, Sabrina," Mr. Moonbeam said.

Storm walked over to Sabrina. "You look just like your mother—enchanting!" The horse walked towards Elliott and said, "It is good to see you, too!"

Elliott patted Storm's head and said, "It is good to see you too, Storm."

Mr. Moonbeam said, "Storm will carry us up the hill to the old mansion." The horse nodded.

With a wave of his wand, Mr. Moonbeam, Elliott, and Sabrina were all lifted by magic onto the horse's back. Elliott held on tightly to Mr. Moonbeam's cloak. Sabrina petted Storm's hair which felt like silk and smelled like the ocean.

A mild autumn wind blew calmly as the silver horse trotted up the hill. Dead rose bushes lined the path to the old mansion. The bony, bare branches of the twisted rose bushes frightened Elliott who thought the branches might reach out and grab him at any minute.

Mr. Moonbeam, the horse, and the children continued up the spooky path until they came to a tall iron gate that towered above them. Storm knelt down and let Mr. Moonbeam and the children off.

After admiring the sad looking willow trees that grew by the gate, Sabrina walked over to the entrance. A sign was posted above the gate.

"What does it say?" Mr. Moonbeam asked.

"I'm not sure. Let me see." Sabrina snapped her fingers and a white flame emerged from her fingertip. Taking a deep breath, she slowly floated up and used her flame to read the sign while Elliott watched in amazement.

STORM'S ADVICE

"It says Mossy Mansion," Sabrina said as she floated back down and blew out her flame.

"I can do that," Elliott said.

Sabrina looked at Elliott and said, "Let's see."

Elliott closed his eyes, waved his wand, and imagined himself leaving the ground. This feeble attempt at levitation was stopped short as Mr. Moonbeam grabbed Elliott's hand before his foot even left the ground.

"We have more important things to do than show off. Remember, both of you will be able to use your magic tonight? Don't worry, Elliott. You'll be able to use your powers soon enough," Mr. Moonbeam walked towards the gate.

The rusty lock would not budge. "I guess we will have to fly over it," he said.

Elliott interjected, "No, let me open it! I can open it with my mind."

The wise old horse walked towards Mr. Moonbeam and said, "Give him a chance, Sloan."

"Okay Elliott, use your mind to open the gate. Concentrate," Mr. Moonbeam backed away from the gate. Elliott closed his eyes and thought deeply. He imagined the gate, but in his imagination, the gate was shiny and new. Then, he imagined the lock slowly coming undone and the gate door swinging open. He held that thought for a moment and opened his eyes. But, to his disappointment, the gate remained locked—nothing had changed.

Sabrina walked over to the gate and stared at the lock. Then, she pointed her finger towards the lock and a burst of fire emerged from her fingertip which melted the rusty, old lock. The creaky, old iron doors opened slowly.

"Now, it's open," she said arrogantly.

Elliott lowered his head in shame.

Mr. Moonbeam walked over and put an encouraging hand on Elliott's shoulder. "Elliott, you gave it your best shot. There will be more opportunities for you to practice your magic tonight."

Elliott looked at Sabrina. Then, he looked at Mr. Moonbeam. "I don't understand. Whenever I want my magic to work, it won't. Then, when I don't want it to work, it does. Can you explain that, Mr. Moonbeam?"

Mr. Moonbeam knew Elliott was frustrated, but he could not answer Elliott's question. Sabrina's ease and talent with magic made the situation worse.

Mr. Moonbeam stood in the moonlight. His bright eyes looked directly at Elliott, "We will fix this Elliott. I promise you that. It is going to take time. After all, I've only been your teacher a few months. I'm still trying

STORM'S ADVICE

to understand you and your magic. Please be patient. Remember, you can learn from watching Sabrina as well. Don't get upset with her."

Elliott looked at Sabrina. "Her? I'm not upset with her. I know a show-off when I see one." Elliott turned his back.

Sabrina walked towards Elliott. "A show-off? I just have natural talent and you are jealous."

"More like a lot of HOT air," Elliott snapped.

Mr. Moonbeam said, "You will develop your magical abilities, Elliott. After all, Sabrina has lived in Moonstone all her life. She was able to practice witchcraft whenever and wherever without hiding it. You've had to hide your powers from everyone except your parents, so she has had a lot more practice than you." Mr. Moonbeam tried to reason with the kids.

"I don't hide my powers from anyone, Sloan," Sabrina commented rudely. "His name is Mr. Moonbeam," Elliott exclaimed.

Mr. Moonbeam waved his wand and everything stopped suddenly. Time stood still for the children. They were frozen—Sabrina with her mouth open—Elliott with his arms folded looking the other away.

"Are you having a difficult time controlling your students, Sloan?" Storm asked sarcastically.

Mr. Moonbeam looked at his horse. "Do you have any suggestions?"

Storm said, "Yes, as a matter of fact, I do." The horse walked closer. "Do you remember my brother, Wind? He could run faster than me. He could jump higher than me. He did everything better than me. He was a true athlete, and I couldn't compete. I was the opposite of what everyone expected a horse to be. I felt worthless for a long time. You made me feel better about myself because you gave me a purpose—to help you and others. *You're going to have to give both of these children a purpose or a reason for magic.* Otherwise, it is just a foolish competition among children."

Mr. Moonbeam thought for a moment. Until now, Elliott and Sabrina were told to practice witchcraft for their own personal reasons, to get better, or just for fun. Storm was right! Somehow, he had to make magic more meaningful for the children.

Mr. Moonbeam looked at his horse and said, "The first step is to regain their respect."

"Exactly," said Storm. "You are the adult. You are their teacher."

Mr. Moonbeam looked up at the moon. His eyes began to glow. His wand became energized as his cape waved behind him.

STORM'S ADVICE

He waved his wand at the children.

"Why don't you just shut up!" Sabrina yelled.

As Elliott was getting ready to say something, Mr. Moonbeam interrupted. In a stern voice he said, "Sabrina, I gave Elliott the task of opening the gate. I wanted to give HIM an opportunity to practice using HIS powers. You took that opportunity away from him, and it was not the right thing to do. You need to show patience and learn how to respect others, no matter how impatient you may feel when someone performs slower than you do. You will call me Mr. Moonbeam when I am teaching you. Is that understood?"

Sabrina's face turned slightly red.

Mr. Moonbeam looked at Elliott. "You must believe in yourself, Elliott. Stop feeling sorry for yourself when you make a mistake. Each mistake is a learning opportunity and life is full of mistakes, or learning opportunities."

Elliott said, "But my magic is always messing up. How can I call myself a witch when I can't even do the simplest spells?"

Mr. Moonbeam put his hand on Elliott's shoulders and said, "You are more than just a witch, Elliott. You are a boy. Remember that. All of this is new to you.

Nothing worthwhile comes easy . . . but trust me . . . your magic will come and it will improve!"

Sabrina looked away while Elliott listened attentively. He trusted Mr. Moonbeam's advice and believed in his words. He wanted to believe that his magic would get better. He wanted to believe that he could be a great sorcerer someday. Mr. Moonbeam's kind encouragement made him feel better.

The wind picked up speed and blew some of the fall leaves in a circle around Mr. Moonbeam, the children, and the horse. They all looked in unison at the creepy, run-down, old mansion that stood before them.

Mr. Moonbeam said, "Tonight, we practice having patience with ourselves and with each other and we will learn from our mistakes."

Elliott smiled. Mr. Moonbeam was in charge again. He felt better when Mr. Moonbeam took the lead.

Sabrina looked annoyed as they all looked at the spooky, old mansion. She was bored with the non-magical world. She wanted to go back to Moonstone.

9

MOSSY MANSION

Mr. Moonbeam, Storm, and the children all walked through the gate. The old mansion stood like a tall, dark, giant in front of them. Beside the grayish, brown house, with its purple shutters, was an old well with a bucket tied to a rope.

Mr. Moonbeam led the children to the porch. Elliott was afraid he might fall through the damaged boards that squeaked beneath his feet. "You'd better stay behind, Storm. This rotting wood might not be able to support your weight," Mr. Moonbeam said. Storm agreed and stood next to the old well.

The old mansion stood like a tall, dark giant in front of them.

MOSSY MANSION

Mr. Moonbeam turned the knob and entered the dusty mansion. Inside, the old house was dark. A beam of moonlight fell on a lantern placed on a table. Mr. Moonbeam grabbed the rusty lantern. He had an idea.

With glowing eyes, he turned towards Sabrina and said, "I want you to light this wick with your eyes."

Sabrina seemed surprised. Furthermore, she was not used to anyone telling her what to do—even a teacher. Suddenly, the wind blew the door shut making the room darker.

"Can I point my finger at the wick?" she asked. The children were scared.

"No. I want you to gaze and illuminate. It might be easier if you included an incantation with your gaze," Mr. Moonbeam suggested.

Sabrina was not used to reciting incantations. Furthermore, she was not good at composing her own poetry. However, the darkness of the old room bothered her. She wanted light quickly.

Annoyed, she stared at the dried, old wick and said:

Wick in the night
Make it bright!

Elliott and Mr. Moonbeam watched as nothing happened. Elliott felt amused but also nervous. He wanted to brighten up the room as well.

Sabrina looked at Elliott and said, "I'll try again."

Mr. Moonbeam nodded.

Sabrina said:

> *This old lantern is dry*
> *Fire come alive!*

Again, nothing happened.

Mr. Moonbeam moved Elliott next to Sabrina and asked, "Have you two ever heard of cooperation?" Sabrina looked away.

He continued, "It's when two people work together to combine their talents. Elliott, you will recite an incantation for making fire. Sabrina, you will focus on the wick and light it."

The children, although resistant at first, agreed to give Mr. Moonbeam's approach a chance.

Elliott looked at Sabrina and said, "Are you ready?"

"Of course, I'm ready," Sabrina snapped. "I'm always ready."

Elliott rolled his eyes.

Mr. Moonbeam watched the children.

Sabrina nodded reluctantly. She wasn't used to working with other children. She focused her witchy gaze on the lantern's wick. Elliott took a deep breath and concentrated on the lantern before saying:

Dry wicks and rusty, old lanterns
Spooky houses with worm-eaten banisters
Tonight, this wick
Will light and shine
For its flame
Shall be mine!

Mr. Moonbeam watched with enjoyment as a flame shot up from the dried wick that had not burned in centuries. Its eerie light brightened the dusty living room.

Jumping up and down, Elliott smiled at Sabrina and said, "We did it! We did it!"

Sabrina said half-heartedly, "It's just a little flame. That's all."

Mr. Moonbeam added, "No, it's more than that. You worked together to solve a problem. You used patience and cooperation and that is an excellent start towards controlling your magic!"

Sabrina had no comment as she looked around the old living room.

Elliott grabbed the lantern and said, "Look at this spooky, old room!"

The living room smelled musty. Mr. Moonbeam looked at the old furniture. He removed some white sheets that covered two old couches and sat down on the torn purple cushions. The dust made Elliott sneeze.

In addition to the couch, there were several coffee tables and a few antique lamps. A large moth-eaten rug covered the floor. On the walls, portraits of people, ghosts from the past, stared back at Mr. Moonbeam and the children.

Elliott walked over to play a few notes on an old piano which was badly out of tune while Sabrina looked at a faded painting of a man and a woman that hung over the fireplace. The man wore a uniform and the woman wore a black dress. Words were written on the bottom of the frame.

"Bring me the lantern. There's something written here," Sabrina said.

Elliott walked towards the portrait and held the light up to the frame.

"What does it say?" Mr. Moonbeam asked.

Elliott said, "It says *General Butler and His Wife Ginny*."

Mr. Moonbeam thought silently for a moment, "Where have I heard that before? Better yet, how does this connect to the Halloween Crystal and Noir? Why did the crystal send them to this old mansion?"

Elliott was surprised to hear Mr. Moonbeam's thoughts. His magic was working!

Elliott and Sabrina watched Mr. Moonbeam's pale face study the portrait. Once again, they saw the look of a young sorcerer—the look of magic. Mr. Moonbeam was thinking. He knew that crystal balls provided vague visions. He did not understand the connection between the vision in the crystal ball and Mossy Mansion.

"Perhaps coming to the mansion was a mistake," he thought. Still, he had to investigate.

Elliott picked up Mr. Moonbeam's thoughts but kept them to himself. He felt embarrassed when his teacher suddenly looked at him.

Then, Mr. Moonbeam noticed the carpeted stairs which were as tattered and torn as the faded wall paper. Although old and decayed, he knew that the neglected old house must have been extremely beautiful in its day. For here it stood in ruins; yet, it still harbored its memories from a time long ago—the portraits, the furniture, the rooms.

Everything reminded him of a different time because the house, although ruined, was in near pristine condition except for the cobwebs, dust, rotted wood, and tattered furniture. It was like an old museum that had been left to stand the test of time. No person from the town of Wolf's End dared to enter the old mansion because it had been considered haunted for many years.

There was a sudden feeling of loneliness as Mr. Moonbeam and the children looked around the old house. It was as if the old couch, with its wooden frame and dingy cushions, longed for General Butler and his wife Ginny who must have sat side by side on the couch centuries ago.

Mr. Moonbeam visualized in his mind what life must have been like for the general and his wife. He could see Ginny Butler and the general sitting on the couch, and he imagined her reaching over to turn on the old oil lamp that was so carefully placed on the old, wooden coffee table next to the couch. Elliott also picked up on these thoughts and all around he could also feel the presence of General Butler and his wife and the life they had lived in the mansion.

In a way, it made Elliott sad to look at the rusty fire poker that rested next to the dusty fireplace—probably put there by the general himself over 200 years ago! Elliott was amazed that even now, after all these years, a single log rested in the fireplace—ready to be lit, ready to be burned—on a cold winter's night.

"Let's go upstairs," Mr. Moonbeam said.

Taking the lantern, he led the children up the staircase to the second floor. Each step sent crackling noises through the air as Mr. Moonbeam tried to avoid any weak floorboards, but it was not easy. The banisters were rotted, too.

Elliott held on tightly to Mr. Moonbeam's cape. Sabrina, who could not help but stare at the portrait, looked back occasionally. Elliott grabbed her hand.

At the top of the stairs, they saw a long hallway lined with thick, wooden doors. The stained wallpaper on the walls was just as ruined as the warped floorboards. All the doors to the rooms were closed.

Sabrina asked, "So now what?"

Mr. Moonbeam who was carrying the lantern answered, "We explore these rooms."

Now, Elliott felt scared. He looked down the spooky, dark hallway at each door that was shut tight. It was as if each door was saying, *"Enter at your own RISK!"* The spookiness made Elliott uneasy, but not Sabrina. Having grown up in Moonstone, she was used to drafty old castles, haunted houses, and creepy old cemeteries. Elliott felt a cold draft of wind. He buried his face in Mr. Moonbeam's cloak. He was ready to go home.

"Wouldn't it be easier to split up?" Sabrina suggested.

"Are you crazy?" Elliott asked as he squeezed his teacher.

"Scared?" Sabrina asked sarcastically. Not only was Sabrina spoiled and selfish, she was also risky, and her boldness annoyed Elliot who was scared to death.

Trying to avoid an argument, Mr. Moonbeam interjected quickly.

"Sabrina may have a point. If we split up, we will save time. We will split up into pairs," Mr. Moonbeam said.

"But there's only three of us," Elliott remarked.

"That's not quite true young man." Mr. Moonbeam reached into his cape and took out a beautiful, white bird. Mr. Moonbeam stood in the dark hallway with the old lantern in one hand and a beautiful white bird in the other. "This is Snowflake," Mr. Moonbeam said.

Sabrina, enamored by the beautiful bird, walked towards Snowflake and said, "She's beautiful."

"How many animals do you have in there?" Elliott asked lifting Mr. Moonbeam's cape.

Mr. Moonbeam smiled, "Here take Snowflake. You can check out the room at the end of the hall." Sabrina had never seen a bird with such crystal, blue eyes.

Mr. Moonbeam continued, "Use your wand to light up the room. Elliott and I will check out this room. But, be very careful."

"She likes you," Elliott said.

"How do you know?" Sabrina asked.

"I read her mind," he replied.

"Can she talk?" Elliott asked Mr. Moonbeam.

Mr. Moonbeam said, "In a way, Elliott. She can communicate with certain people. Those who can read thoughts, like yourself."

Elliott seemed pleased to have a talent that separated him from Sabrina. He suddenly realized that his magic worked well in the old mansion, but he didn't know why.

"What's Snowflake saying now?" Sabrina asked urgently.

"She wants a cracker," Elliott giggled.

As the magical teacher and his two students stood in the spooky, cobweb filled hallway, Mr. Moonbeam reached into his pocket and gave the bird a cracker. They all watched the bird eat the cracker by the light of the lantern. It was a nice moment despite their spooky surroundings.

10

A HAUNTED MANSION

I

ELLIOTT AND MR. MOONBEAM ENTERED one of the rooms located in the middle of the hallway. The cold, icy hand of a ghostly draft met Mr. Moonbeam as he slowly opened the squeaky door. Each creaking floorboard sent a shiver down Elliott's spine.

Inside, dusty books lined the shelves of an old library. Mr. Moonbeam turned up the lantern and set it down on a large wooden table in the center of the room.

"Look at all these books!" Elliott said.

Mr. Moonbeam commented, "Untouched for a hundred years. Amazing!"

"So what are we looking for?" Elliott asked.

Mr. Moonbeam said, "I'm not sure, Elliott. Your mom saw this house in the Halloween Crystal, so there is something important here. There is some connection between this house and Noir wanting to steal the Halloween Crystal. For all we know, he might be in this house right now, in disguise.

Mr. Moonbeam worried for a moment. Perhaps, he should not have left Sabrina and Snowflake alone.

"Well, I wouldn't know him if I saw him. I've never seen him before," Elliott walked towards the dusty books.

The room itself, though smaller than the living room, was large and once again Mr. Moonbeam could visualize in his mind the way the library must have looked centuries ago. There were beautiful wooden bookshelves built directly into the four walls. While some of the books crumpled to the touch, the bookshelves were solid and built to last!

Mr. Moonbeam walked over to one of the large windows. The panes of glass were cracked but still intact. Down below he could see Storm resting by the old well under the light of the moon. Indeed, Mr. Moonbeam thought the old house was truly beautiful despite its neglect and decay.

Mr. Moonbeam began to survey the dusty books that lined the shelves. He picked up an old book and was surprised when it crumbled in his hands.

11

SABRINA WALKED INTO AN OLD BEDROOM with Snowflake perched on her shoulder. She used the purple star on her wand to light up the room. Inside, she saw an old lavender canopy bed with sheets and the canopy still intact, a chest of drawers, a nightstand with an old green antique lamp, an old purple rug, and a wardrobe closet. An open window with a torn curtain caught her attention and she watched as a leafless willow tree swayed in the wind.

"Well, I have to admit. I'm a little scared, Snowflake." She looked at the closet in front of her. "Do you think we should look in the closet?" Snowflake tilted her head.

She walked towards the wardrobe and opened the door. A cold wind blew through the room ruffling the canopy which was covered in dust and cobwebs. Inside the closet there was an oval mirror with a sturdy frame.

A large, gray spider disappeared quickly behind the mirror as Sabrina wiped the dust and looked at her reflection. The antique mirror still looked beautiful—protected for centuries—in the wardrobe closet.

A foggy haze in the background of her reflection caught her attention in the mirror. She turned around but saw nothing. Then, she looked in the mirror again and the mysterious haze came back. One more time, she turned to look behind her, but nothing was there.

Sabrina turned her face towards the mirror again and watched the mysterious haze form an outline which took on the shape of an old face, and she realized she was staring at a ghost! She looked at Snowflake. Then, she turned back towards the mirror.

She recognized the ghostly face. It was the same person she had seen in the portrait downstairs in the living room. It was Ginny Butler. She opened her mouth to scream, but nothing came out.

III

"HEY! LOOK WHAT I FOUND!" ELLIOTT turned towards Mr. Moonbeam.

A HAUNTED MANSION

"What is it Elliott?" Mr. Moonbeam asked.

"It's an old book. I found it in this drawer. It looks like an old diary or journal." Elliott sat the book on the table next to an old globe.

Mr. Moonbeam skimmed through the book and said, "This diary might be the reason the crystal sent us to this old mansion. Good for you! Your mind led you in the right direction."

Once again, Elliott made note of the fact that, for whatever reason, his powers seemed to work better in the old mansion.

Elliott smiled at his teacher, "Can we go home now?"

Mr. Moonbeam said, "Yes! Let's get Sabrina."

Placing the book inside his cape, Mr. Moonbeam led the way towards the door, but on the way to the door, Elliott tripped on a rug.

"Are you okay, Elliott?" Mr. Moonbeam asked.

"There's something under this rug," Elliott said.

Mr. Moonbeam helped Elliott get up. He moved the lantern closer to the floor. Under the rug, there was a trap door.

"Should we open it?" Elliott asked.

Mr. Moonbeam looked worried.

IV

SABRINA AND SNOWFLAKE STARED AT THE ghostly figure in the mirror.

Like a dream, the ghostly white face spoke softly in a raspy whisper, "Come closer, child. Move closer to the mirror."

Sabrina took a step closer to the mirror. Any closer and she would have been inside the closet. She looked at the ghost and asked, "Are you the ghost of Ginny Butler?"

The ghost said, "Yes, I am. Yes, I am. Do you recognize me?"

Sabrina said, "Yes. I saw you in the portrait downstairs."

The ghost moved closer and said, "The one with my husband, the general?"

Sabrina nodded.

The ghost mumbled, "So sad . . . so . . . so sad."

The ghost sighed. Her haunting voice became rougher, "You are in terrible danger, child. Do you know that Noir, the dark sorcerer, wants to kidnap you? He wants to take you back to Moonstone."

Sabrina said, "I love Moonstone. I'm not happy here. I need to be around magic. I miss my castle."

The ghost nodded, "Of course you do, of course you do, but your mother sent you here so that Sloan Moonbeam could protect you. Isn't that right?"

Sabrina nodded, "Sloan is my mother's friend."

The ghost chuckled, "Yes, yes, I know all about that. Now, let me tell you something very important. Are you listening?"

Sabrina nodded and moved closer while Snowflake, who had been sitting on Sabrina's shoulder, fanned her wings nervously.

V

MR. MOONBEAM PLACED THE LANTERN ON the floor and opened the trapdoor. He lowered the lantern into the opening, and a cold, earthy draft blew out the flame.

"Let's get out of here, Mr. Moonbeam. I have a bad feeling...."

But, before Elliott could finish his sentence, he was pulled through the trapdoor's opening. Mr. Moonbeam grabbed Elliott, but the pull was too powerful. It pulled both of them inside a tunnel that seemed to fall through a hidden wall in the old mansion.

They fell into complete darkness.

Mr. Moonbeam reached for his wand, so that he could light up the tunnel. However, before he could do anything, they landed abruptly on the ground.

"Ouch!" Elliott said.

"Hold on Elliott. I've got my wand," Mr. Moonbeam took out his wand and waved it in the air. With one wave, hundreds of tiny sparkles lit up an underground cellar.

"Wow! Why didn't you do that before?" Elliott asked.

"Never mind, let's get out of here," Mr. Moonbeam answered.

"But where do we go? Sabrina is all alone in the house!" Elliott said.

Mr. Moonbeam noticed Elliott's concern. He looked at the floorboards above them. They were covered in delicate cobwebs. Somehow, they had fallen through a secret passage that ran through the walls from the second floor to the cellar of the old mansion.

The huge cellar was dark and damp with a dirt floor. Shelves filled with hundreds of jars lined the brick walls of the cellar. Mr. Moonbeam walked over to one of the shelves and picked up a dusty jar and examined its contents. Elliott walked over to look.

"What does it say?" Elliott asked.

A HAUNTED MANSION

"It says *Invisibility Potion, Lilac and Lavender.*" Mr. Moonbeam opened the jar which was sealed tightly and smelled the potion.

"It smells like flowers," Elliott said. Mr. Moonbeam nodded. He looked at all the jars.

"No doubt these are the magical herbs and potions that belonged to Ginny Butler hundreds of years ago," Mr. Moonbeam said.

They walked through the cellar and admired the magical items all around them. Indeed, Elliott had never seen so many magical herbs. He tried to read as many labels as he could: mistletoe, St. John's wort, snakeroot, sunflowers, foxglove, and holly to name a few. But there were also jars of seawater, rainwater, and one with dead fireflies.

He held up the jar of fireflies and thought, "I guess they must have been alive once . . . "

At the end of the tunnel there was a large table covered with wooden wands. Mr. Moonbeam picked up one of the wands and examined it. Then, he laid it down on the table next to some feathers and stitches made from a coarse yarn.

At the end of the tunnel, there were three dark passage ways covered in cobwebs. "Let's take one of these tunnels," Mr. Moonbeam said.

He started to enter one of the tunnels when Elliott said, "No, not that one!" Elliott pulled Mr. Moonbeam's cape.

"You have a bad feeling about this one?" Mr. Moonbeam asked.

Elliott nodded.

Mr. Moonbeam said, "Well, then you lead the way, Elliott."

Elliott grabbed the lantern from Mr. Moonbeam's hand and headed towards one of the three tunnels. Mr. Moonbeam noticed hundreds of bats staring at them from the ceiling. Their eyes glowed like tiny mirrors in the darkness of the passageway. He was worried about Sabrina.

VI

UPSTAIRS IN THE OLD BEDROOM, WITH ITS dusty canopy bed, Sabrina stood in front of the closet and stared at the ghostly face in the mirror. The ghost spoke and Sabrina listened:

> *Do as I say*
> *Do as you are told*
> *You will listen*
> *To those around you*

A HAUNTED MANSION

You will learn
From those you know
For, all they know
Will be yours to know
Just look in a mirror
And, my face
You will see
Then, all you know
Will be mine to know.

Like melting snow crystals, the ghost's pale face faded away slowly and Sabrina felt different. She felt sleepy. Her eyes felt tired. She wanted to go home. With Snowflake perched on her shoulder, she turned in a daze to leave the haunted old bedroom. She walked towards the door and stopped.

Outside, the bony hand of a willow tapped at the window. She turned and looked. She listened to the tapping for a minute before leaving the room.

VII

MR. MOONBEAM AND ELLIOTT FOLLOWED THE tunnel which took them to a door and a set of stairs that led them to an abandoned garden outside the mansion. There was a brick path that led from the cellar stairs to the center of the garden. Mr. Moonbeam and Elliott stood in the center of the overgrown garden.

While the leaves of the trees were now autumn colors, Mr. Moonbeam knew that the garden must have been a sight-to-see in the summer months. For all around them were a variety of bushes, shrubs, and trees used for magical purposes. Mr. Moonbeam, who was not a magical botanist, knew enough to recognize and appreciate the magical diversity present in the trees that grew in the garden. As Mr. Moonbeam and Elliott walked through the garden, he saw birch, alder, ash, apple, yew, poplar, holly, and willow trees, and he knew that it was from these trees that Ginny Butler had made the magical wands which rested in the cellar of the house.

Elliott, amazed by the magic of the fall evening, looked towards the well and saw Sabrina standing next to Storm in front of the house.

"Sabrina! You made it out of the house!" Elliott ran from the garden towards Sabrina. Mr. Moonbeam, who had been examining an oak tree, turned and ran towards the children.

"I looked for you and Mr. Moonbeam, but I couldn't find you. So, I came outside. Mr.

A HAUNTED MANSION

Moonbeam, I'm tired. Can we go home?" Sabrina asked.

"Yes. I know you are both tired. Did you find anything in the bedroom?" Mr. Moonbeam asked Sabrina.

"Just an old mirror—that's all," Sabrina yawned. "Did you two find anything?" she asked. Mr. Moonbeam took the diary out of his cape and showed Sabrina what they had found, but she didn't really pay any attention to it.

Elliott felt dizzy for a moment. "Mr. Moonbeam, I don't feel so good."

"I think we are all tired," Mr. Moonbeam looked at the children, the house, and the garden. "What does all of this mean?" he thought. He had no idea, but he knew that it was time to go home. He also knew that he would return—at a later time—to fully explore the secrets of Mossy Mansion.

"We can fly home. It has been a long night," he said.

Mr. Moonbeam reached inside his cape and pulled out his broom. He walked towards Storm. With a flick of his wrist, he shrunk the horse down to size and carefully placed him in his pocket. Then, he opened his cape and Snowflake flew inside.

"Amazing," Elliott commented.

Mr. Moonbeam hopped on his broom, and the kids

hopped on too. In an instant, they took off leaving a trail of sparkles behind them.

Sabrina looked back at the mansion. She felt changed, but she was not sure why. It bothered her.

The force of the wind made Elliott's eyes water. He looked at the moon. Then he looked down at the ground. The spooky old mansion and its garden disappeared from sight. He admired the trail of sparkles that followed the broom as it sailed through the night sky. He closed his eyes and fell asleep.

11

HALLOWEEN IS IN THE AIR!

THE NEXT MORNING AT BREAKFAST, Elliott told his mother everything about Mossy Mansion.

"Mr. Moonbeam has the diary. It's a very old diary. It was written by a woman named Ginny Butler," Elliott said while cutting one of his pancakes.

His mother replied, "People in town talk about that old house a lot."

"Are you talking about the house on Rose Hill?" Elliott's dad asked as he sat down at the table.

"Yes, Mr. Moonbeam took us there last night. I found a diary written by a woman named Ginny

Butler. Mr. Moonbeam kept the diary. He didn't want to wake you up, so he tucked me into bed. He wanted me to tell you that he would be over this evening." Elliott drank his juice.

"Did you say Ginny Butler?" Christian asked.

"Yes," Elliott replied.

"Have you heard of her?" Greta asked.

"Yes, I have," Christian answered.

"Who was she?" Greta seemed interested.

"No time to talk about it now." Christian looked at his watch.

Elliott put his books in his backpack. "I'm so glad that tomorrow is Halloween!"

"Let's go, Elliott," his dad said. Like Mr. Moonbeam, Elliott's dad had a job in the non-magical world. He worked at a library.

The drive to school was mostly silent. From the car, Elliott admired the crisp fall morning and all the houses decorated for Halloween. The decorations and the magic of the season made him happy to be a witch.

"It's too bad we can't use magic around non-magical people, dad. I love being a witch," Elliott said.

"It's against the rules, Elliott. Things are different in Moonstone," Christian said.

HALLOWEEN IS IN THE AIR!

"Moonstone sounds awesome," Elliott said. He smiled and thought about how great Moonstone must be. He imagined himself casting spells on dragons and flying through enchanted forests. He imagined himself reading minds and casting invisibility spells.

Then, he thought about Noir and his vampires and monsters. Suddenly, the idea of a real vampire seemed frightening. His feelings about Moonstone had changed.

His father pulled up beside the school, and Elliott saw a group of kids playing in a pile of leaves. This made him feel better.

"Goodbye dad. I'll see you tonight," Elliott said. He kissed his dad and ran towards the school.

Once inside, he could not believe the Halloween decorations in the hallways. He stopped to read the Fall Festival posters. There would be games like *Bobbing for Apples* and *Wrap the Mummy*. He could not wait because this was going to be an awesome Fall Festival!

All around, the students were talking about Halloween and the plastic skulls, rubber bats, bendable monsters, spooky rubber balls, creepy erasers, and other prizes they had won at last year's Fall Festival. Elliott had won a goldfish in a bowl—which he kept as a pet.

Last year's festival was a lot of fun for Elliott and his friends. They ran up and down the hallways in their costumes without getting into trouble. And all the teachers dressed up too. Elliott's mom even came dressed up as a witch! Of course, only Elliott knew that she was actually a REAL witch.

When Elliott walked into his noisy classroom, he could not believe his eyes.

"Wow!" he exclaimed.

Mr. Moonbeam had put up more Halloween decorations. Purple spiders and black bats hung from the ceiling and every student had a plastic jack-o-lantern on their desk. But the biggest surprise of all was the huge pumpkin sitting on Mr. Moonbeam's desk.

Lucas walked up to Elliott and said, "Aren't these decorations cool?"

Elliott looked inside the plastic jack-o-lantern on his desk. He found a vampire eraser.

"Hey, look! I got a vampire eraser!" he showed Lucas.

"I got a mummy," Lucas showed Elliott his eraser.

"Are you going to the Fall Festival?" Elliott asked.

"Yes, I'm excited. Some kids are going to paint their faces for the festival. Are you?" Lucas asked.

"I'm not sure. Hey, what if I ask my mom if you can stay all night? Do you want to?" Elliott asked.

HALLOWEEN IS IN THE AIR!

"Sure! You can call me after school," Lucas said.

"I will!" Elliott said.

At that moment, Mr. Moonbeam walked into the room and all the kids yelled his name.

"Do you like the decorations?" Mr. Moonbeam asked as the students ran towards him cheering. He smiled. It felt good to celebrate with the kids. It made him happy to be a teacher. It was impossible for him to address each question or respond to each cheer from the jumping children that swarmed him. So, he just smiled and said, "Yes . . . I think so . . . sure . . . "

After the class quieted down to complete an assignment, Mr. Moonbeam called Elliott to his desk.

Mr. Moonbeam whispered, "Did you tell your parents that I would be over this evening?"

"Yes. My dad knows all about Ginny Butler. Where is Sabrina?" Elliott asked.

"She didn't feel well this morning. Storm is watching her. I think she caught a cold or something," Mr. Moonbeam said. "Were you tired this morning?" he asked.

"No! I'm too excited about Halloween," Elliott exclaimed.

"It will be here soon," Mr. Moonbeam said smiling.

"So, your dad knows all about Ginny Butler?" Mr. Moonbeam asked.

Elliott nodded and said, "I'm going to ask my mom if Lucas can stay all night tonight."

Mr. Moonbeam replied, "Are you sure that's a good idea? After all, I'll be at your house. Remember the rule. Witchcraft must remain a secret."

"Don't worry. We'll just stay in my room and play. Lucas isn't nosey at all," Elliott smiled. "He's a quiet kid."

"Oh, I see," Mr. Moonbeam ruffled Elliott's hair. "We will let your mom decide. Now, you'd better go back to your seat. It is time for math," Mr. Moonbeam said.

Elliott walked back to his desk. He smiled at Lucas. He smiled at Mr. Moonbeam. He loved Halloween. He loved school.

12

MOONSTONE

MOONSTONE IS A MAGICAL WORLD—not another planet—more like another dimension closely intertwined with the earthly non-magical world. Some magical beings are chosen to live a non-magical existence, interacting with non-magical people, in the non-magical world. Others live a magical life in Moonstone. Wherever they live, these witches, warlocks, traveling gypsies, sorcerers, wizards, and magicians all have one thing in common—magic.

Enchantra is Moonstone's most powerful witch, and she rules over this magical world. Centuries ago, she named her island, the Island of Orange and Blue.

Her castle is guarded by the orange and blue mermaids that live in the lush, green kelp beds that surround her island. It is an island paradise, and the orange and blue mermaids protect Enchantra from Noir and his red and black dragons.

Noir and many other evil sorcerers and witches live among the hags, vampires, werewolves, ghosts, and monsters that haunt the Dark Lands. This scary place is the home of Noir's vicious red and black dragons. These fierce, flying, fire-breathing dragons have the power of invisibility. They soar high above the dark trees often landing on the balconies of the castles scattered throughout this eternally dark, mountainous region of Moonstone. They fan their wings and shoot balls of fire into the night sky. Noir controls the dragons and monsters in the Dark Lands with his dark magic.

Because of this, Moonstone is not always a peaceful kingdom of small cottages, enchanted castles, and wooden gypsy wagons scattered across an enchanted countryside. There is a constant battle between good and evil magic, and the effects of the Magical Civil War, fought centuries ago, still linger throughout Moonstone.

Moonstone changes with the seasons. In the winter, this magical world becomes cold and icy. Because there's no electricity in Moonstone, people burn fires to stay warm. They read by candlelight and cook on wood burning stoves. They store their food in old root cellars. In the spring, the witches and gypsies of Moonstone walk through the forests looking for wildflowers and herbs. They use these herbs to season food and make magical potions.

Summer days mean trips to magical lakes, rivers, and oceans. During the summer, people open the windows and doors of their cottages and castles to enjoy lazy days and warm breezes. They work in their gardens and cool off in their root cellars. They walk the grassy countryside to visit neighbors, relatives, and friends. They sit under shady trees and discuss potions and spells while the children play games. Life is nature and nature is life.

In Moonstone, autumn is the most MAGICAL time of the year! At night, the enchanted cottages and castles situated throughout the countryside glow from the candles that burn in every window. Children place lit jack-o-lanterns on door steps, hearths, and in attic windows to scare off evil spirits. Scarecrows with arms that flail in the wind protect acres of corn from the crows that fly overhead. Every night people celebrate the joy of the season with bonfires, parties, and food.

During this time of year, it is not uncommon to see a traveling gypsy wagon parked alongside a country road. Young witches and wizards often stop to have their fortunes told. Some become so enchanted by this experience; they decide to become traveling gypsies themselves and join enchanted carnivals. Others set up fortune telling booths in towns by the sea.

Elliott's parents and Mr. Moonbeam were chosen by Enchantra to be guardians and live among non-magical people. Syballine, however, did not accompany Mr. Moonbeam and the others to the non-magical world. She stayed behind.

Dressed in black, she stood on her balcony and gazed at the fields that surrounded her white castle. The night air smelled of autumn herbs. She watched the scarecrows dance in the wind. Their arms waved like wild skeletons. All around her, the magic of the season captured her heart, but something was wrong. She could feel it and it worried her.

She walked inside her castle and grabbed her bag of tea leaves. She poured the leaves into a dish and examined them. As she watched carefully, certain disturbing visions began to unfold.

She noticed Sabrina's face in the tea leaves. In the vision, Sabrina looked sad. She turned the dish slightly left and saw a ghostly face she did not recognize. This bothered her. Finally, she turned the dish once more and recognized the dark shadow of Noir.

Placing the dish on the table, she walked out to her balcony. She gazed at the moon in the distance. She looked up at the stars. She would travel tonight to see Sloan and Sabrina. She was worried.

13

NOIR

THE SORCERER DRESSED IN RED TRIED to tame the wild dragon with his whip. "Back down! Back down! Into the cage! Get into the cage!"

The red dragon did NOT want to be caged. He breathed fire at the sorcerer and showed his razor-sharp teeth. Odin pointed his ruby tipped wand at the roaring dragon.

"Perhaps my black magic will change your mind," he said. However, he was stopped immediately.

"What is the meaning of this?" Noir asked standing in front of the dragon.

"This dragon needs discipline," Odin said lowering his staff.

"Not today!" Noir shouted.

He walked towards the dragon. Under his witchy stare, the dragon became tame and playful. Noir used his mind to tell the dragon to fly.

The dragon raised its head and let out a huge fireball. Then, the red dragon fanned its powerful wings and flew away. Noir watched the dragon fly into the dark sky towards the dark clouds and the full moon.

"They are beautiful creatures." His wicked eyes sparkled.

He turned abruptly, "You will never treat my dragons like that again. Do you understand?"

"Yes, master," Odin seemed irritated but agreed nonetheless.

Noir and Odin lived in the darkest part of Moonstone, the Dark Lands.

The pair crossed the moat of dark water that surrounded the enormous red and black castle nestled in the mountains. This castle, the darkest in all of Moonstone, stood as a testament to Noir's great power. It was a huge castle with many balconies, turrets, and cone shaped steeples that towered over the Dark Lands. While the castle itself was ink black, its many narrow windows were illuminated blood red—a direct correlation to the color of Noir's many dragons.

In the Dark Lands, the eternal songs of the trees and their leaves were haunting melodies that drifted in the wind. It was a sad metallic song that sounded like leafy chimes crying in the night.

Noir and Odin entered the castle and made their way through the elegantly decorated corridors and hallways to an enormous stone flight of stairs that traversed in a zigzag manner through the many floors of the castle. Their footsteps echoed as they walked up the winding stairs to a floor with a green and black checkered hallway that seemed to extend for miles.

The evil pair passed the ghostly portraits and candles that hung on the walls until they came to a door that led to a bridge that extended from one wing to his ghostly lair—the highest point of the castle. They crossed the bridge and entered Noir's chamber.

Noir walked past his magical mirrors, his plush throne, and his glittering jewel case to his balcony. A ghostly magician dressed in black, he watched the clouds move slowly across the moon. He listened to the trees and their soft songs. Werewolves howled in the distance. Ghostly figures rose up into the night. It was time for his creatures to haunt the Dark Lands.

The white interior of his black cape flashed in the moonlight as he walked back inside towards his throne and his wooden case filled with enchanted jewels. These black and blue jewels that glistened were the source of his magical powers.

He took a sparkly blue gem out of the case and walked towards a large mirror brightened by candlelight.

"Ginny, Ginny Butler, come to me," he said in a deep voice.

He held the glowing blue gem in his hand.

From behind, Odin watched as the ghostly appearance of a witch who had lived centuries ago formed in the mirror.

"Halloween is almost here, Ginny," Noir said.

"I know. I know," the ghost replied in a raspy voice. "Do you feel the spirits? They are restless." Ginny said nervously.

"Indeed, I do," Noir replied. He walked around the room admiring his sparkling jewels. His cape flowed.

"It's a pity that you are no longer alive, Ginny. I know how much you miss Moonstone, riding around on your broomstick, cooking with magical herbs. It must be so sad to be a ghost. I know how much you want your revenge," he tempted the spirit.

"So sad, so sad," said the circling ghost.

Noir's eyes twinkled. He looked in the mirror, "But, I can change all of that, remember? *Remember, what I promised?*"

The ghost moved in the mirror, "Yes, I do. Yes, I do. I did what you asked. I did what you asked."

Noir looked pleased, "Good! So, you were able to put a spell on the girl."

"Yes, yes, so sad, so sad," Ginny's ghost looked sad. "How long will I wait? How long?" asked the ghost. She looked at the sparkly blue gem in Noir's hand.

"On Halloween night, you must wait until Halloween," he promised the ghost.

"Must wait, must wait," the ghost said. "What about my husband?" The ghost rubbed her ghostly hands together nervously.

"Were you able to locate him on the ghostly side?" Noir asked the ghost.

"So lost, so lost," the ghost replied moving in circles.

"That's too bad. It seems your husband is lost forever," Noir said sarcastically.

"NO, NO, NO!" Ginny's ghostly screams echoed throughout the castle.

Ginny's face became bigger as her ghostly white body moved in circles. Noir backed away from the mirror. He laughed, and his laughter echoed throughout the Dark Lands. The werewolves and vampires stopped to listen.

The ghost settled down, "You will find him? You will find him?"

Noir turned away and placed the blue gem in the sparkling case of jewels next to a huge, glowing, black diamond. "When your work is completed, I will find him. I must wait and see if Sabrina can lead me to the Halloween Crystal. Then, the deal will be finished. Syballine's daughter is special. She might be able to break the spell."

"No chance of that. No chance of that," echoed the ghost.

Noir said, "Enough for now. You may go, Ginny. Remember you are the face in the mirror. You must look for the girl and keep the spell alive."

"So sad, so sad," said the disappearing ghost.

Noir turned towards Odin and said, "Sabrina will help me find the Halloween Crystal. Then, I will have the power to enter the other world on Halloween night. With the crystal's power, I can rule both worlds. It is only a matter of time until Enchantra loses her hold over Moonstone's witches. It is only a matter of time."

Noir laughed and his sinister voice echoed throughout the castle. The mirror remained empty. The blue gems glistened in the dark, velvet case. The large, black diamond glowed.

14

GINNY BUTLER'S DIARY

ONCE AGAIN, MR. MOONBEAM WAS GOING to Elliott's house to discuss the Halloween Crystal, Noir, and the haunted house on Rose Hill. Elliott was excited because Lucas was coming to stay all night.

After arranging his favorite toys, games, and model cars neatly on his desk, Elliott ran downstairs.

"Is Sabrina coming too?" he asked his mom who was busy using magic to rearrange furniture.

"I'm not sure Elliott. If she does, you will all have to stay in your room and play. No kids downstairs tonight and ABSOLUTELY NO MAGIC! Do you understand?" Elliott's mom was serious.

Elliott nodded, "I know mom. Don't worry. Lucas is a nice, quiet kid. He isn't nosey at all. We'll just stay in my room and build models."

Elliott's mom smiled. "That's a good idea. I like Lucas. But, don't forget about Sabrina. She might get bored watching you boys build model cars and buildings. If she gets bored, it would be nice for you boys to play games instead."

Elliott agreed and ran back upstairs. He wanted to make sure he was ready for his friend.

Elliott's parents sat down on the sofa.

"Are you going to tell me about Ginny Butler?" Greta asked.

Elliott's dad said, "Well, I don't know a lot. She lived here over 200 years ago and married a sea captain. Her husband was not a warlock, and she got in a lot of trouble by the witches council for marrying outside of magic. The captain built the old house on top of Rose Hill for Ginny, and they lived there for many years. Later, people in the town accused Ginny of witchcraft and they executed her. Her husband died a lonely old man."

Elliott's mom was amazed. "I've never heard of this story."

"Not many witches have. She married outside of

witchcraft and never returned to Moonstone. She must have lived a sad life," Elliott's dad said.

A flash of lightning shined through the window. He walked over to see. "There's a storm brewing outside. The leaves are really blowing off the trees," he said.

"But, you don't know that," said Greta. Christian looked surprised, "Don't know what?" he asked.

Greta continued, "Maybe she wasn't sad. Maybe she loved her non-magical husband."

Christian said, "Oh . . . we're still on the subject of Ginny Butler. Well, I suppose that's possible. Still, she was unable to return to Moonstone. Don't forget that."

There was a knock at the door. Greta walked to the door and was greeted by a flurry of leaves blowing in the wind. After a few words with Lucas' mother, she led him upstairs to meet Elliott.

"Elliott. Lucas is here," she opened his bedroom door and left the two boys alone. When she got downstairs, she was surprised to see Mr. Moonbeam, Syballine, and Sabrina in her living room.

"I didn't know you were coming, Syballine," Greta said as she hugged her guests.

"I was worried about Sabrina," Syballine said. The rumbling sound of thunder shook the house.

"I'm okay, I just have a little cold," Sabrina said. She looked at Elliott's parents.

"Elliott and Lucas are playing upstairs, Sabrina. Do you want to go upstairs?" Greta asked.

"Sure, why not. I'm kind of bored," Sabrina said. She walked upstairs to meet the boys while Elliott's parents, Mr. Moonbeam, and Syballine sat down to talk.

"I'm sorry Sabrina comes across as being rude and spoiled. I guess it is my fault. I am hoping that you can help her, Sloan. But, it seems that Sabrina is unhappy living in this non-magical world. Today, the tea leaves showed me some disturbing visions," Syballine looked worried.

Mr. Moonbeam sat down. Since Lucas was a guest in the house, none of the witches changed into their magical clothes.

Mr. Moonbeam said, "Sabrina missed school today. She has been acting strangely since visiting the old mansion on Rose Hill. She swears that nothing happened to her inside that house, but I have a strange feeling that..."

Syballine stood up and said, "You left her alone? How could you do that, Sloan? You were supposed to protect her!"

Mr. Moonbeam answered, "I know. I realize I made a poor decision, but I was trying to teach the children how to work together and also be independent. I sent Snowflake with Sabrina."

Elliott's mom asked, "Who is Snowflake?"

Mr. Moonbeam snapped his fingers and Snowflake appeared on his hand. A sudden flash of lightning illuminated the mysterious bird.

Syballine looked at the bird. "I can't believe that you left Sabrina alone in that house. This bird couldn't have protected her from Noir's magic should he have entered this world." Snowflake fluttered her wings.

Mr. Moonbeam said, "Once again, I apologize Syballine, but I was trying to teach the children independence and responsibility. After all, Noir cannot enter this world completely without the Halloween Crystal. There was no real danger."

Elliott's dad said, "I think we need to move this conversation to the Halloween Crystal and discuss the old mansion. What did you find, Sloan?"

Mr. Moonbeam discussed the picture of Ginny and her husband as well as the library and the book that Elliott had found. Christian told the group about Ginny Butler and her life as a witch in the non-magical world. Mr. Moonbeam placed Ginny's journal on the table.

"Let's take a look at the old book," Elliott's dad suggested. He picked up the book and found most of the pages old and illegible, but there were a few pages he could read aloud.

GINNY'S DIARY

*I*T HAS BEEN TWO LONG YEARS *since my last visit to Moonstone. The other witches are terribly jealous of me and my life with the captain. I can feel it in my bones, so I've decided to live a non-magical life. Once Enchantra found out, she was terribly upset with me. Especially, since I had been chosen to live secretly among non-magical people. However, I've told the general about Moonstone and my powers. I broke the most important rule of all . . . I told a mortal that I am a witch!*

Enchantra reminded me of my place among witches and reminded me that it was an honor to be chosen to live among non-magic folk as a secret guardian. She talked about my wilted gardens and my responsibility to teach the others how to brew magical formulas. "Ha! Ha!" I said to her. "Let them find their own way. They want to steal my

GINNY BUTLER'S DIARY

husband. They want my life—my love. I will not go back to Moonstone."

With that, I left Moonstone for good. My husband built me a beautiful house and named it Mossy Mansion. When he is at sea, I tend the gardens and grow wild herbs, but these herbs are nothing like my magical beauties in Moonstone.

Most of the time, I'm happy here. But, I do miss my gardens. I miss flying at night, scanning the fields, watching the scarecrows dance in the wind. Someday, I will have my revenge on Enchantra. She claimed to have taken all my powers, but that's a lie! Little does she know... I have one special power left....

Christian looked at the others, "That's where it leaves off. It seems that Enchantra knew Ginny Butler when she was alive."

Syballine looked concerned, "Then we must summon Enchantra again and ask her why the crystal sent us a vision of that old house."

Mr. Moonbeam said, "Enchantra may not even know how Ginny Butler is connected to all of this, but one thing is certain, she IS connected to all of this."

Greta added, "But, how is that possible? Ginny Butler has been dead for more than 200 years. She was executed as a witch. How could she be connected to Noir wanting to steal the Halloween Crystal?" The steady sound of raindrops hitting the house filled the room. Greta shut the window.

Christian said, "Noir's powers are strong. If Ginny Butler knew Enchantra, then she would be very valuable to Noir. But, we must remember that only the noblest witches are chosen to interact with non-magical people."

Mr. Moonbeam looked at Syballine. "And Ginny Butler broke the most important rule. She fell in love with a non-magical person and divulged her true identity as a witch. It sounds to me like she would be a perfect accomplice for Noir, as a ghost."

They all looked at one another. Outside, the wind picked up speed. On the mantle above the fireplace, three glowing jack-o-lanterns stared back at them.

15

A CONFLICT AMONG FRIENDS

Sabrina grew tired of watching the boys build model cars. Without magic, life seemed dull and boring to her.

Lucas held two tiny pieces in place while Elliott tried to glue them together. She watched him struggle to hold the pieces with steady hands.

"What a waste of time," she thought to herself. "That would be so easy with magic."

Sabrina increased her concentration, and by magic, the two pieces joined together with no effort at all from the boys.

"Hey!" Elliott turned towards Sabrina.

"I'm bored," she said walking towards the window.

Lucas did not seem to notice the magic that had just taken place before him, but Elliott did. He grabbed Sabrina's arm and took her down the hall into his parent's bedroom.

"What's the big idea? You know we can't use magic in front of non-magical people. Lucas is NOT a witch!" Elliott said.

She sat down on the bed. "Who cares? What are you going to do? Are you going to tell my mom? She's downstairs. Go ahead!"

Elliott felt like he was going to lose control of his powers. "You know what's wrong with you? You . . . you . . . you are a spoiled BRAT!" He snapped. "And no one likes you—especially us!"

Sabrina crossed her arms and turned her head. "Go back to your stupid models and your boring friend. Leave me alone."

He stormed out of the room with his heart beating fast and bumped into Lucas. "Come on. Let's go back to my room. Who needs her?" He slammed the door behind them.

Sabrina walked out into the hallway. The sound of the autumn rain mixed with the crackling thunder left her feeling cold and alone. She thought about going downstairs. She could tell her mom that she wanted to go back to Moonstone, but her mom had made it clear that she was not to be bothered.

She walked into the bathroom and shut the door. Tears fell from her eyes. She reached for a tissue and looked at herself in the mirror when a strange feeling suddenly came over her. She had felt it before. It was the same feeling she had felt at Mossy Mansion. The memories she had forgotten suddenly became real again as she looked into the mirror.

"Hello, child," said the ghost of Ginny Butler.

16

THE POWER OF INVISIBILITY

Sabrina stared vacantly into the mirror as the ghostly figure asked, "Do you remember what you must do?"

"Yes," she whispered. "Everything will be yours to know, but I know nothing."

"Yes . . . yes . . . yes . . . I know, child. I know," the ghost chuckled. "But you will know more . . . much, much more . . . in a few minutes."

Sabrina looked deeply into the mirror. Nothing else mattered. She had forgotten about Elliott, her feelings, and her frustrations.

"You know, my dear. Right now, downstairs, they

are discussing the Halloween Crystal. Right?" asked the ghost.

"I think so," Sabrina answered.

"Good . . . good. That's what we want. Do you see the bottle over there?" Ginny pointed to a lavender bottle on the sink.

Sabrina looked at the bottle. "Yes," she said.

"Drink it. Drink it," whispered the ghost. "It has special powers."

She reached for the bottle, removed the cap, drank the liquid, and gazed into the mirror.

Ginny's raspy voice said, "Look at your hands child. Look at them."

Sabrina raised her hands but saw nothing. Her hands were gone. Everything was gone. The sudden sound of thunder scared her.

"I'm . . . I'm invisible," she mumbled.

Ginny laughed, "Yes . . . yes . . . you are. Yes . . . you are. Now, go downstairs, child. And spy . . . spy on them. Tell me what they know. Remember, what is yours to know is also mine to know . . . now go . . . go . . . "

Sabrina stood frozen. "You have no choice, child," said the ghost. "Do not resist."

A strange feeling came over Sabrina. She felt compelled to go. Like a dream, she walked slowly out of the

THE POWER OF INVISIBILITY

bathroom and down the hall. She stood at the top of the stairs and listened. A wicked smile formed on her face.

She crept down the stairs and walked into the living room. She stared at Mr. Moonbeam. He did not see her. None of them saw her.

Mr. Moonbeam said, "It is certain and we all know it. The closer we get to Halloween, the more certain I am that Noir is closing in. It is only a matter of time."

Syballine spoke, "Then we need a protection spell, and we need it immediately!"

Mr. Moonbeam said, "You could be right, but protection spells are short lived. There are so many things that we are unsure of—Ginny Butler, Mossy Mansion, and their connection to the Halloween Crystal."

Sabrina walked closer towards Mr. Moonbeam. She no longer felt like a ghost in a daze. She was alert and wanted information. She was on a mission.

She smiled at her invisibility and felt powerful knowing the others could not see her. She walked towards the lighted jack-o-lanterns and waited for Mr. Moonbeam to speak.

"We need to understand Ginny's connection to all of this," Mr. Moonbeam said.

"If we had the crystal, I could gaze into it and ask the questions we want answered. After all, it led us to

Mossy Mansion. It might give us more detailed clues," Greta said.

Sabrina smiled. They were closer to telling her what she wanted to know.

Christian said, "That's too dangerous. Enchantra said it must remain hidden, and I do not think we should go against her advice. Besides, listen to that storm outside!" He walked over to the window.

Syballine said impatiently, "We have no choice but to go to the clearing tonight. We need to summon Enchantra. She knew Ginny Butler when she was alive and she might know the reason why the crystal sent us to her mansion."

Greta said, "You two go ahead. We will stay here and watch the children."

Syballine replied, "It was a bad idea letting that boy come to your house tonight. I don't feel like myself dressed in these non-magical clothes. The situation is dire and we need to act now." She paced nervously around the living room.

Sabrina sat on the floor in front of the fireplace. She listened to the rain. She watched the lightning through the window. She smiled to herself. She would wait . . .

Mr. Moonbeam said, "Summoning Enchantra would be pointless. She doesn't know why the crystal

THE POWER OF INVISIBILITY

sent us to Mossy Mansion to find Ginny Butler's journal any more than we do. Crystals provide clues—that's it. The Halloween Crystal is special. It affects those it comes into contact with. It sends mixed messages. It speaks half-truths. It has a dark side too."

Standing up, Mr. Moonbeam restated what Enchantra had said, "Only the purest heart should ever touch it."

Syballine turned and breathed deeply, "I never touched it." She looked at Mr. Moonbeam.

"What are you saying, Syballine?" Mr. Moonbeam asked.

Sabrina smiled a half-smile and breathed deeply.

"Is it playing games with you, Sloan? Why are you so reluctant to summon Enchantra?" Syballine asked impatiently.

Mr. Moonbeam looked at her, "Because Enchantra can offer us nothing. She doesn't know why the crystal led us to Mossy Mansion. It is a mystery. But one thing is not a mystery, this is personal for you, and you are starting to panic."

There was a moment of silence. Syballine looked at the others. "Well, you would panic too. Don't tell me you wouldn't." She looked at Greta and Christian.

"How would you feel if it was Elliott? If he was . . . If Noir was Elliott's father?" She put her face in her hands and wept. Greta walked over and sat next to her.

"We will never be free. My daughter and I will never be free," Syballine cried.

Sabrina watched her mother and wanted to say something, but she could not bring herself to say anything. She fought back a feeling. What was the feeling? What was she talking about? She didn't know what it was. She stood up and walked towards her mother and thought about what her mother had said.

"Noir is my father?" Sabrina thought about it for a moment and almost came back to reality, but the spell was too powerful. She couldn't control her thoughts and her feelings. What did she feel? Was it sorrow? She was not sure because what she felt was masked by something stronger—an insatiable need for *ONE PIECE* of information. The tears that streamed down her mother's face meant nothing to her. She was under a spell. All that mattered was the crystal because *THAT WAS THE PIECE OF INFORMATION*. But, where was it? She felt impatient . . .

Greta spoke, "I'm sorry Syballine. We all understand, and we are your friends. You have nothing to worry about. The crystal is hidden safely in the river. No one could ever find it—especially Noir."

And with that sentence, Sabrina smiled to herself. Her task was halfway complete. She sighed deeply, crept out of the room, and walked out of the back door into the autumn storm.

Elliott ran down the stairs and yelled, "Mr. Moonbeam! Sabrina is gone! She ran away!"

17

THE FIGHT BEGINS

WHEN MR. MOONBEAM SAW THE LAVender bottle on the bathroom sink, he knew the truth. He knew that Noir had managed to reach Sabrina.

"It is an invisibility potion," Christian said. "I can smell the lavender residue."

Mr. Moonbeam said, "But who put it here? Elliott do you know?"

Elliott looked scared and frightened. "We got into an argument. Sabrina used magic in front of Lucas, and I . . . I took her into mom and dad's bedroom and I told her she was a spoiled brat."

Syballine looked at Elliott, "And what happened next?"

Elliott thought for a moment, "I went back into my room. I didn't want Lucas to hear. I didn't want him to know about the magic."

Greta spoke, "Elliott, I'm going to have to take Lucas home for the night. Things here are too . . . "

"Come here, quickly," Mr. Moonbeam interjected. He was looking in the mirror. "Do you see what I see?" he asked the others.

Deep within the mirror, Mr. Moonbeam saw the hazy outline of something. He was not sure exactly what it was.

Greta also looked into the mirror. She used her crystal gazing powers to look beyond—to find the answers only a gifted gazer could see.

"It's a face. It's a person. But who?" she asked.

The others looked closely in the mirror. They could not see what Mr. Moonbeam and Greta could see. Elliott tried to see.

Christian said, "Elliott go get Lucas. I'm going to take . . . "

Elliott spoke, "It is Ginny. That's Ginny Butler." At that moment, everything became clear. They knew that Noir had used Ginny Butler to place a spell on Sabrina.

THE FIGHT BEGINS

"Using the potions from the cellar in Mossy Mansion, no doubt," Mr. Moonbeam thought as he remembered the hundreds of jars filled with magical items in the cellar of Mossy Mansion.

There was little time. They all knew where Sabrina was headed. She was headed for the river to get the crystal so that she and Ginny's ghost could bring Noir into the non-magical world.

Mr. Moonbeam stood outside the house and looked through the scattered storm clouds at the moon. His eyes glowed. His hair became shinier. With a wave of his hand, his clothes changed. Dressed in black, he stood before the others wearing his boots, his cape, and his magic top hat.

Everyone except Greta changed into their magical clothes. Christian's daggers glowed through his cape, and Syballine's dark hair blew wildly under her witchy hat. They stood in the breeze as the rain fell like mist on their faces.

They decided that Greta should stay behind with Elliott and Lucas.

Greta said, "Be careful, Christian. Once you are all gone, I'm going to take Lucas to his mother's house, and then Elliott and I will join you."

Christian said, "No, it is too dangerous. Take Lucas

home and then wait here." Greta agreed reluctantly. She was worried about them, but she needed to take Lucas home.

Mr. Moonbeam said, "We don't have time to fly. We must go now!" So, he waved his hand and they were instantly transported to the river.

Mr. Moonbeam, Syballine, and Christian stood on the dark, rocky beach. The storm stopped suddenly but the sky was still cloudy. All around them, dark pines swayed in the autumn breeze. A gentle wind shifted the clouds, and like a thick blanket, they covered the moon.

Mr. Moonbeam felt weaker during moments when the clouds covered the moon. Christian spoke, "The crystal is here, right here. I'll swim down and see . . . " But before he could finish his thought, a sinister laugh echoed towards them.

The misty rain caused the wind to become colder. Mr. Moonbeam wrapped his cape around his body as he and the others watched Noir and Sabrina walk towards them. His eyes fell on the Halloween Crystal. The luminescent pearl shined brightly in Noir's hand.

Syballine called for Sabrina but there was no answer only the sound of thunder and the flashes of lightning behind the trees.

THE FIGHT BEGINS

Suddenly, Mr. Moonbeam raised his hands above his head and moved them in circles. At the same time, he stared at the moon, and purple rays of light emerged from his hands. He aimed his purple, magical energy at Noir.

Syballine and Christian did the same. Their white and green magic joined Mr. Moonbeam's powerful rays of purple magic, and this energy whizzed like a knife towards Noir. Their magic cut through the darkness of the storm while the misty rain stung their faces.

However, Noir held the Halloween Crystal up against the magical energy that beamed towards him, and the crystal absorbed the magic with an unbelievable force.

The drizzle that fell from the clouds drenched Sabrina as she watched the battle in front of her. She watched her mother fall to her knees and cry. She watched the others trying desperately to defeat Noir. The crystal was draining them of their magic, and they were clearly tired. She wondered how long this magical battle would last.

Then, as quickly as it had started, the battle stopped, and Mr. Moonbeam, Christian, and Syballine fell to the ground silently, exhausted of all their powers. There was only the sound of the rain as Noir grabbed Sabrina's hand and walked towards them.

Holding the crystal towards the sky, he looked at Mr. Moonbeam, "Thank you, Sloan. Your powers have energized the Halloween Crystal. Its dark side is more powerful now thanks to ALL of you." His wicked face flashed in the lightning.

Mr. Moonbeam, too tired to say anything, struggled to get up. His wet hair covered his eyes. He longed for the moon's energy which was now blocked by dark storm clouds. He wrapped his cape tightly around himself as he managed to get up. He did not know it but Elliott and Greta had both appeared at the scene on their brooms. As they landed, Elliott watched wide-eyed as Syballine walked towards Noir and said, "Please, Noir, please . . . just give her to me. Take the crystal, but give Sabrina to me."

Noir ignored Syballine's plea. He stood by the child while his cape blew in the wind and said, "Today, I take what is rightfully mine, the Halloween Crystal, and my daughter!"

Mr. Moonbeam spoke up, "She's under a spell—a spell that you helped to create."

"I see you finally figured it out. It took you long enough, Sloan," Noir said sarcastically. With each word, the thunder grew louder, and the rain poured harder.

THE FIGHT BEGINS

Mr. Moonbeam said, "Only YOU would DARE make a deal with a tormented ghost. You are playing with spirits, Noir. You are playing a dangerous game." Mr. Moonbeam felt the moon's energy start to revive him. Noir sensed this, so he pointed the Halloween Crystal towards the moon and a large group of clouds covered its light.

He said, "It is pointless, Sloan. Even your powers are no match for the crystal's energy. And this is only a fraction of what it can do."

He walked towards Mr. Moonbeam. "On Halloween night it will be done. Both Moonstone and this world will be mine and I will put an end to this Magical Civil War once and for all. You cannot stop me!"

Mr. Moonbeam said, "We will stop you."

Noir looked directly into Mr. Moonbeam's eyes and said, "And on Halloween night, when the veil between the two worlds is paper thin, I will use the crystal to take ALL that is mine and open a portal into this world, so that my monsters can conquer all of this for ME!"

His sinister laughed echoed behind the thunder and his dark features became highlighted by the lightning.

Noir's eyes darkened. He stared at Syballine and held the crystal towards the sky. One of his red and black dragons flew down from the storm and landed by the river. It roared so loudly that Sabrina shivered and screamed. Noir grabbed her and together they floated up onto the dragon's back. The dragon carried them off into the storm, through the clouds, and Noir's laughter echoed throughout the river valley.

Syballine buried her head in her hands and cried.

The rain poured as Mr. Moonbeam clenched his fists. His eyes glowed as he stared at the moon.

18

ELLIOTT'S VISION

STANDING NEXT TO THE RIVER, MR. Moonbeam placed his head in his hands. The moment seemed to last forever. As Syballine wept for the loss of her daughter, Mr. Moonbeam thought about his terrible mistake. How could he have left Sabrina alone in Mossy Mansion with only a bird for protection? What had he been thinking? But it wasn't just Sabrina, Mossy Mansion, and Ginny Butler's ghost that went through his mind; he also thought about his responsibility as the lead guardian—chosen by Enchantra—to protect the non-magical world as well as those he was asked to serve.

This battle was over and all was quiet except for the sound of the river. It had stopped raining. While the moon shined brightly among the dark clouds, Mr. Moonbeam felt weak and exhausted from fighting Noir. Greta and Christian helped Syballine get up. They started to comfort her. Elliott walked quietly towards his teacher.

"Are you okay, Mr. Moonbeam?" Elliott asked.

Mr. Moonbeam looked at Elliott. It was hard for him to say anything. Elliott was safe. He was with his parents and his teacher. But, where was Sabrina? Most likely, Noir was headed back to Moonstone to plan another attack. Where would Noir attack next?

Mr. Moonbeam looked at Elliott and asked, "Do you think Sabrina will be all right, Elliott?"

Elliott was surprised by the question but his instincts told him that Sabrina was okay. All was not lost. "It's not over, yet, Mr. Moonbeam. I think she will be okay."

Mr. Moonbeam listened to Elliott's words and looked at the others who were also watching the scene. He walked over to them and looked at Syballine. Her eyes were red from crying.

"We are going to get Sabrina back. We are going to stop Noir. We need a plan," he said.

Christian said, "Let's go back to the house and sit down and figure out what to do next. There isn't much time."

ELLIOTT'S VISION

They all agreed and together the five witches headed back to Elliott's house on their magic brooms. Once inside, everyone sat down, except for Mr. Moonbeam. He paced nervously back and forth. The others could tell that he was agitated.

Mr. Moonbeam said, "I have to go to Moonstone. Noir will attack the villagers and take over Moonstone. Then, on Halloween, he will use the crystal to open a portal to this world at the stroke of midnight."

Greta said, "Then we will all go with you, Sloan. You can't defeat Noir alone."

Mr. Moonbeam said, "For now, I think you should all stay here. I need to see Enchantra."

He bowed his head and the others felt sorry for him.

Syballine walked over to him and placed her hand on his shoulder. She said in a quiet voice, "You did your best, Sloan. It's not over yet. We all let Enchantra down. We all played a part in this. Sabrina's my daughter. Perhaps I should have done better . . . as a parent."

While the adults talked, Elliott suddenly felt his mind wander off to thoughts that had nothing to do with the conversation happening before him. He walked over to the fireplace and his eyes became fixated on the fire as certain images came to his mind. At first, he wasn't sure what was happening, but then he realized that his magic was working. His magic was sending him visions, thoughts, and feelings. He concentrated on the fire while the adults talked.

What was he seeing? He wasn't sure, but a bright moon illuminated the vision and Elliott was able to see clearly as his mind wandered further away from the non-magical world. Indeed, Elliott had never seen such beautiful mountains, hills, and valleys. The valleys, surrounded by tall mountains, stretched for miles. Elliott saw small cottages scattered throughout the many valleys. Each cottage was illuminated brightly by candles that burned in opened windows.

Then the vision shifted and Elliott saw acres and acres of dried cornstalks in large fields decorated with scarecrows and pumpkins. The beautiful images made him smile and his mind's eye wanted to see more.

Like a low flying plane, Elliott's vision moved beyond the cottages, beyond the autumn fields and tall mountains, to a beautiful ocean with water so clear it sparkled in the moonlight. He continued to smile when suddenly the scene shifted and Elliott felt fear like he had never felt before. He winced as a huge red and black dragon flew before his eyes.

For a moment, Elliott came back to the conversation in the living room. He could feel his heart beating

ELLIOTT'S VISION

quickly as he thought about the dragon that had suddenly appeared in his vision. What was it? What did it mean? His parents and Mr. Moonbeam were busy discussing the plan.

He focused his gaze on the fire again and saw hundreds of red and black fire-breathing dragons. They were headed towards a small island. At the front of the dragon cavalry was a dark, scary man. The man's cape blew in the wind as he rode the fiercest, largest dragon among all the other dragons. Behind him, Elliott saw Sabrina. Her face was expressionless. Her mind seemed blank. He felt scared and sad for her.

Elliott saw the dragons descend on the small island. In the moonlight, their fires reflected on the water as they burned up the beautiful trees that outlined the island. Suddenly Elliott saw beautiful orange and blue mermaids jump out of the ocean— each one holding a spear or a trident. The mermaids plunged their weapons into the dragons' chest. Elliott watched as several dragons, stabbed to death, fell to their watery graves. But he also watched many of the beautiful mermaids get hit by the powerful tails of the dragons—flung back into the sea. The battle was a whirlwind of destruction that also sent hundreds of mermaids to their watery graves.

The fire-breathing dragons spewed flames towards the mermaids who were protected by their shields. Elliott had never seen anything like it. The mermaids could swim. They could jump. They could stop, suspended in mid-air, and fight the dragons that breathed fire. Elliott watched the dark leader steer his large dragon towards the beautiful white castle that the mermaids were trying to protect. But, it was too late. The large dragon aimed its gigantic flame towards the drawbridge and burned it up immediately.

Elliott watched Noir and Sabrina enter the castle. He felt sad for Sabrina and the hundreds of dead mermaids. Their lifeless bodies floated down to the murky depths of the green kelp beds they had worked so hard to take care of. Elliott watched Noir point the Halloween Crystal towards a noble, wise looking witch wearing a beautiful golden dress. With the crystal in his hand, Noir approached Enchantra's throne. Elliott could hear his sinister laugh.

He turned towards the others and yelled, "Noir has Enchantra! Her island has been destroyed."

The adults in the room looked at Elliott with surprise.

But, Mr. Moonbeam grabbed his broom. And in an instant, he left the others. Elliott walked to the window

ELLIOTT'S VISION

and looked outside. A trail of sparkles was all that remained of his teacher's path.

Moonstone is a vast world. This drawing shows a part of Moonstone.

19

MR. MOONBEAM'S RESOLVE

MR. MOONBEAM DIDN'T HAVE TIME to think about Elliott's improved mental powers. He didn't finish his conversation or finalize his plans with the others. He knew the vision that Elliott received was an accurate vision. He should have known that Noir would attack the Island of Orange and Blue. He should have known that Noir would capture Enchantra. It was part of Noir's quest for unlimited power and part of his plan to destroy everything good and beautiful in both worlds.

Mr. Moonbeam flew over the sleepy town of Wolf's End to the magical pathway between the two worlds.

Once he crossed over into Moonstone, he felt different. He felt at home.

He charged his broom and forced it to fly at lightning speed. As dawn approached, he looked at the moon and watched it fade away. But he didn't feel tired. The moon's rays had energized him.

As Mr. Moonbeam crossed through worlds it was as if he had crossed through a warp in time. All around him the magic of witchcraft carried him into a new place where magic ruled. He was home. He was in Moonstone.

He looked down at the magical valley and felt a sense of resolve begin to emerge. Was he defeated? Or was he motivated? He wasn't sure. But, when he saw the first burned cottage he felt different. And then another... and another... It was a path of destruction like he had never seen. Cottages burned to the ground by Noir's dragons. The cornfields burned. The beautiful fall valley was no longer orange, yellow, and brown. It was now charred and burned.

He watched the villagers hug one another in the early morning light. Mr. Moonbeam knew that the villagers were asking each other questions. What happened? Why did this occur? What was going on in Moonstone? Why so close to Halloween? And again,

MR. MOONBEAM'S RESOLVE

Mr. Moonbeam felt guilt overwhelm his soul as he thought about the villagers and all of Moonstone. After all, he had been chosen to protect the Halloween Crystal and keep it from Noir. Mr. Moonbeam had failed.

These feelings bothered Mr. Moonbeam as he forced his broom to go even faster towards the mountains. He flew swiftly through the charred ruins of the cornfields. The scarecrows no longer flailed their arms in the autumn breeze.

After the fields, Mr. Moonbeam came to the large mountains that ran along Moonstone's coastline before the sandy beaches and Moonstone's ocean. Mr. Moonbeam could smell burning grass, leaves, and trees as he flew over the mountains towards the ocean. He knew that the Island of Orange and Blue had been destroyed. Pushing his broom as fast as it could go, his eyes began to water. Soon enough he came to the island and looked down as large fires burned.

Mr. Moonbeam landed softly and stood on the sandy shore of the island. The beach was littered with hundreds of dead mermaids—some still clutching their weapons. He looked towards the burning castle—now in charred ruins.

The pain in his chest caused Mr. Moonbeam to let out a scream that echoed throughout the island, but he was alone. Even the small animals that had once lived peacefully with Enchantra and the mermaids were gone—not even an owl or a seagull remained.

Mr. Moonbeam used magic to lift tons of sand into the air like a sand tornado. This left a large hole on the beach. Then, he used magic to place each mermaid gently into the large hole, or grave. When it was done, he used magic to cover the grave with rocks and sand. His hair blew in the wind as he stood at the large grave. His pale face formed an outline in front of the morning sun.

After a few moments, he walked towards the burned castle. Mr. Moonbeam thought about his childhood days. He remembered that his parents had once brought him to the Island of Orange and Blue during the summer. That was when he had met Enchantra for the first time . . .

"You can expect great things from him," Enchantra said looking at the young boy.

"Thank you great, Enchantra. Sloan is a special boy and we are trying hard to raise him right," said Mr. Moonbeam's mother.

"He may be a guardian someday," Enchantra remarked.

And it was true. Sloan Moonbeam had worked his way up the ranks of magic to become a guardian of both

MR. MOONBEAM'S RESOLVE

Moonstone and the non-magical world. Years of educational study and practice had gotten him this far, but no amount of education, witchcraft, or training had been able to stop the evil destruction that surrounded him. No amount of training or education had prepared him to fight the evil forces that threatened both worlds. At least, that's how he felt.

Walking towards Enchantra's throne, Mr. Moonbeam was once again transported back to his childhood.

"He will be given great gifts," said Enchantra.

Mr. Moonbeam's parents looked confused. They didn't really know what Enchantra was talking about.

"What do you mean?" asked his mother. "We are only simple villagers. We have powers of our own but they are nothing compared to yours and the guardians of Moonstone. How could our son possibly have great gifts?" his mother asked.

Sloan looked up at his mother and father. Then he looked at the noble, Enchantra. She seemed so wise and powerful and his parents seemed so simple.

"It is not for me to say. He will realize his own magical destiny, but I know that he will do great things. You see, it is here. It is here in my crystal." Enchantra pointed to a glowing crystal, placed in a wooden stand, next to her throne.

MR. MOONBEAM AND THE HALLOWEEN CRYSTAL

Mr. Moonbeam's parents looked at the crystal. Inside, they saw a vision of their son, but not as a boy—as a man—dressed in a black suit and top hat waving a magic wand. For at that moment, the young Sloan Moonbeam tried to get a look at his magical destiny but Enchantra stopped him.

She used magic to levitate the Halloween Crystal into the air and said, "You cannot see your own future child. Just remember to study, practice your magic, aim high, and always listen to your parents. They are good people."

But now, Mr. Moonbeam looked at the charred remains of the wooden stand which usually held the Halloween Crystal and felt enraged. He kicked the stand and thought about the crystal which was now in Noir's hands. He became angrier.

He twisted his body and held his wand high and pointed it towards the gaping hole in the castle's ceiling. Like purple lightning, a burst of magic hit the morning sky and immediately turned everything cloudy and gray. Within seconds, rain poured all over the island. The fires went out and everything, including Mr. Moonbeam, became soaked.

He sat down on one of the steps that led to Enchantra's throne and rested for a minute. His dark

MR. MOONBEAM'S RESOLVE

hair formed wet circles around his forehead. He had to think. He had to plan. What should he do next?

He needed to gather the guardians? He needed to meet with the villagers. He needed a solution to this problem. Today was Halloween which meant he had to stop Noir before midnight. Moonstone had already suffered, but he had to make sure that non-magical people did not learn the truth about Moonstone and his world. He had to stop Noir from entering the non-magical world at midnight.

Thoughts raced through his head. As Mr. Moonbeam struggled to find a starting point, his gaze shifted towards a mirror on the wall. Once clear, it became hazy and a figure appeared. Mr. Moonbeam walked towards the mirror and recognized the ghost of Ginny Butler.

"Sloan Moonbeam," the raspy-voiced ghost said. "Come closer, Sloan Moonbeam. Come closer so that Ginny Butler can see you . . . so sad . . . so sad."

Mr. Moonbeam inched closer to the mirror. His cape blew in the wind. The rain poured and soaked him even more, but he didn't care.

20

A BARGAIN

WITHIN THE CHARRED REMAINS OF the castle, behind Enchantra's throne, Mr. Moonbeam watched as the ghostly face of Ginny Butler emerged slowly like a white, hazy puzzle of glittering diamonds. All around, the cool rain which beat down on his head extinguished the fires, leaving behind the smoky charred remains of the once beautiful castle that was now open to the night sky.

"Do you know me?" the ghost asked.

Mr. Moonbeam nodded and said, "You are the ghost of Ginny Butler . . . exiled from Moonstone 200 years ago."

The ghost extended a fist through the mirror and yelled in a haunting voice, "For love, for love, Sloan Moonbeam . . . for love!"

Mr. Moonbeam inched away from the ghostly fist that was a mere haze. "It is partly your fault Ginny Butler that this magical civil war has gone on for two centuries. And now Noir is ready to destroy all of Moonstone."

The ghostly face circled the mirror laughing.

Mr. Moonbeam said, "And you were responsible for Sabrina being captured by Noir and now he is threatening to conquer both worlds. You provided the entryway into the non-magical world. You were the bridge between the worlds and now Noir can spread his dark magic through the Halloween Crystal." Mr. Moonbeam became angry.

The raspy voice spoke, "So sad . . . so sad . . . such a liar . . . a liar!" The ghostly voice echoed throughout the ruined castle.

Mr. Moonbeam moved closer to the mirror. He looked at the ghost and asked, "Who lied to you, Ginny Butler?"

The rain slacked a little as Mr. Moonbeam's hair fell in wet clumps all around his forehead.

The ghost said, "Noir . . . he lied to me. So sad . . . so sad . . . He promised me my husband. I helped him, but he . . . he couldn't give me back my husband. So sad . . .

A BARGAIN

so sad." The ghost buried her white, hazy face in her misty hands and wept.

Mr. Moonbeam felt sad for the ghost, but he didn't trust her at all. He was still angry.

"I'm sorry. I can't help you. I need to clean up the mess that you helped to create." He turned to walk away but the raspy voice called him back.

"I offer you a bargain," the ghost said.

Mr. Moonbeam turned back and gazed at the mirror. With his broom in his hand he said, "I don't make deals with ghosts. It could be a trap. It could be a lie. You are no better than Noir."

The ghost said, "But I know how to win. I know how to beat Noir even though he holds all power—the Halloween Crystal."

Mr. Moonbeam stood there for a moment. Soaking wet, defeated, he did not know what to do. There was no plan in place. Should he trust Ginny Butler? After all, she had caused so much trouble already.

Despite this, Mr. Moonbeam felt that Ginny was sincere. He knew the ghost was desperately holding on to a life from long ago. He couldn't help but feel sorry for the misty face that looked pleadingly into his eyes.

He asked, "What kind of bargain?"

Ginny said, "I offer you the Halloween Crystal for my husband."

Mr. Moonbeam thought for a second, "Why don't you get the Halloween Crystal by yourself? Why do you need me?"

The ghostly face grew large and enraged, "Sloan Moonbeam . . . foolish Sloan Moonbeam . . . Ginny needs Sloan . . . Ginny can't steal . . . Ginny has only mirrors . . . mirrors!" Ginny's voice got louder and the castle shook. The mirror cracked.

Mr. Moonbeam waved his fist at the mirror and said, "I don't make deals with ghosts—especially angry ones!" He walked away with his broom in his hand when he heard the ghost weep. He stood outside the castle and looked at the dark storm.

He felt the ocean breeze on his white face and listened to the pitiful weeping of Ginny Butler's ghost. He couldn't stand it any longer—the ruins stretched out before him—the weeping ghost behind him that longed to be reunited with the soul of her long-lost love—all the pain and heartache that Noir had created. He walked back into the castle.

"I'll do it, Ginny Butler. If you help me, I'll help you." And with those words the deal was sealed and Ginny exchanged a ghostly handshake with Mr. Moonbeam.

21

A GHOSTLY PLAN

As if in a dream, Mr. Moonbeam zoomed from the ruined castle into the sky. He navigated through the lightning and storm clouds that he had created. He flew over the ocean. The misty rain caused him to squint as he traveled faster and faster.

Below him, he saw several fishing boats bobbing in the waves. One of the villagers waved at him and he waved back. All of the villagers of Moonstone needed his help. He needed to help them before Noir enslaved them.

He crossed the ocean and the Western Mountains and tried not to look at the smoldering fires in the valley. It was hard to turn away from the burned-up cottages and charred cornfields that were always so beautiful every Halloween. He smelled the smoke. It consumed him and made him angry. He had to help them. He had to help the people. His mind became focused on that one thought.

He also thought about everything that had happened. For Mr. Moonbeam, flying on a broom provided a time to think. His thoughts went back to his classroom. He wished he was teaching a lesson or decorating the room for Halloween, but instead he was faced with a battle . . . a battle for Moonstone . . . a battle to protect the non-magical world. He had to rescue Sabrina and retrieve the Halloween Crystal. He would help Ginny Butler. It was the right thing to do. After all, her bargain wasn't bad. And as he flew, he went over the plan in his head. With Ginny's help, he would pull it off. He would save both worlds, rescue Sabrina, defeat Noir, and return the Halloween Crystal to Enchantra—if she was still alive.

While Mr. Moonbeam felt overwhelmed with responsibilities, he took comfort in knowing that he had friends to help him. Even Ginny Butler's bargain gave him hope. He would meet with the others at Syballine's castle. That's where he was headed.

A GHOSTLY PLAN

Mr. Moonbeam whizzed over a section of corn fields that were not burned. He smiled when he thought about Elliott because Elliott made him happy. And, Elliott made him feel good about the situation. He wondered why? What could Elliott do? Mr. Moonbeam knew that Elliott didn't even have control of his own magic. Still, a complete sense of happiness came over him when he thought of Elliott.

Mr. Moonbeam looked down at Syballine's scarecrows. Their arms moved wildly in the wind and the jack-o-lanterns that dotted the hillside and valley below were illuminated by magical flames. The stormy sky made the illuminated faces of the jack-o-lanterns more vivid. He was happy to see Syballine's white castle in the distance—untouched by the dragons—still standing proudly among the fields in front of the dark sky.

He landed softly on one of the tall white towers and walked down the spiral stairs to find the others talking loudly while Elliott stared at the adults with a frightened look on his face.

Mr. Moonbeam walked over and put his hand on Elliott's shoulder. "Everything's going to be all right Elliott. Don't worry. I've got a plan."

"Mr. Moonbeam! You're back!" Elliott hugged his teacher. The others turned to look at Sloan Moonbeam. They all hugged each other.

"So, what do we do?" Christian asked.

Greta, Christian, Syballine, Mr. Moonbeam and Elliott all stood around the fire that burned in the fireplace of the old castle. In the middle of the fire, a bubbling cauldron sent soft trails of steam up the chimney. Four adult brooms and one child's broom leaned against the fireplace.

"I made a bargain with Ginny Butler. She can help us," Mr. Moonbeam said. The others were speechless.

"Are you mad?" asked Syballine. "You mean the same Ginny Butler, the same ghost that helped Noir kidnap my daughter."

Mr. Moonbeam expected Syballine to be angry. He knew the idea of collaborating with Ginny Butler was preposterous, but somehow, he had faith in Ginny and believed that she could help. So, he explained the conversation that he had had with Ginny Butler. Elliott listened to Mr. Moonbeam tell the story and he could picture it all in his mind—Enchantra's ruined castle, the pouring rain, the ghost in the mirror behind Enchantra's throne, and Mr. Moonbeam standing there soaking wet, listening.

A GHOSTLY PLAN

The ghost said, "It's a bargain. I'll help you get the girl and the crystal, if you help me reunite with my husband."

Mr. Moonbeam looked confused and said, "But I can't help you do that. I have no idea how to find a lost spirit—let alone one that's been gone for 200 years."

Ginny laughed a raspy laugh and said, "That's okay, Sloan Moonbeam. I know . . . yes, I know . . . but you see . . . the answer is right in front of you . . . " The ghost chuckled and moved in circles in the mirror.

Mr. Moonbeam moved a wet strand of hair from his forehead and said, "I don't understand, but tell me now, and don't play games with me, or I'll leave. Time is running out. I need to get back and stop Noir before midnight. Today is Halloween!"

"Yes, Halloween . . . Halloween . . . Halloween," the ghost chuckled. "Come closer Sloan. Come closer to the mirror so that I can tell you a secret."

Mr. Moonbeam hesitated. With his wand in his hand he leaned closer to the mirror. Up close, Ginny looked human. He could see that outline of her human face within the white, misty haze that made-up the ghostly reflection. He felt sad for the ghost as he clenched his jaw and listened, alert, ready for anything.

Moving in circles, Ginny Butler's ghost said:

For don't you see..
A bargain for a bargain..
I help you, you help me..
And from beyond the grave..
You will see..my husband..the captain..
Will come back to me..
For the power is right there, Sloan Moonbeam
It's in the crystal of Halloween . . .

Elliott and the others listened intently. He could visualize it in his mind. He felt somewhat afraid but admired the courage that Mr. Moonbeam exuded while telling his ghostly story about how he could use the Halloween Crystal to reunite two old souls.

"What happened next, Mr. Moonbeam?" Elliott asked. The others listened too.

Mr. Moonbeam continued by telling the others that he realized that Ginny Butler had explained what he and the crystal could do for her, but she still hadn't explained how she would help him.

"Enough of this nonsense, you've told me nothing except what I can do for you. I'm leaving this place before you waste any more of my time." Mr. Moonbeam turned away when suddenly Ginny's bony hand rested on his shoulder.

A GHOSTLY PLAN

"No wait . . . for you see . . . I can help you get through the many dark hallways of Noir's castle. I can help you steal his most powerful jewel, *the Dark Diamond of Disappearance and its connection to the Dark Star*," Ginny laughed.

Mr. Moonbeam knew about the Dark Diamond of Disappearance and its connection to the Dark Star.

The diamond served as a magical gateway to the Dark Star a place where Noir would be lost. Noir kept the black diamond in his castle, hesitant to use the magic himself, for it was very powerful and any witch who chose to use its dark magic could accidentally be exiled to the Dark Star.

Mr. Moonbeam thought for a moment and said, "If I had the diamond."

Ginny interrupted, "Yes! Yes! Sloan Moonbeam, you could use Noir's own magic, from his own dark diamond, to make him disappear—forever!"

Mr. Moonbeam said, "But I'd have to sneak into his castle and steal the diamond, and I would have to get the Halloween Crystal out of his hands before I used the Dark Diamond, or the Halloween Crystal would disappear with Noir."

Ginny's ghost listened. "I can help you get through Noir's castle, Sloan Moonbeam. An image of Noir's black castle came to the mirror. Mr. Moonbeam had never seen such a large castle."

Ginny spoke, "For you see, the castle has many hallways and mirrors and I know all about mirrors. I can get you through the castle and its mirrors . . . yes."

Mr. Moonbeam knew that there was a risk of being captured or lost forever in Noir's dark castle which was filled with magical monsters, hidden entrances, trap doors, and other obstacles. But Mr. Moonbeam knew that the Dark Diamond of Disappearance would give him a way to banish Noir from Moonstone. He had to take the chance.

"You can figure it out, Sloan Moonbeam. You can figure out how to get the crystal away from Noir for just a split second so you can use the Dark Diamond of Disappearance to send him off into the void of the Dark Star forever," the ghost laughed.

Mr. Moonbeam looked at the ghost and agreed. He extended his strong pale hand and shook hands with the ghostly, bony hand that extended itself from the mirror—sealing a partnership in magic.

This was the first step in implementing his plan to defeat Noir and save Halloween.

22

TRUTH SEE'ER

THE OTHERS STOOD BY THE FIREPLACE in the beautiful, old castle and stared at Sloan Moonbeam. He looked at his friends, and he knew. He knew that they probably thought he was crazy. Making a deal with a ghost? Forming a partnership with the same ghost that helped Noir capture Sabrina? Using dark magic to rescue Sabrina and Enchantra? Using dark magic to retrieve the Halloween Crystal and save both worlds? It was all risky.

Syballine was the first to speak, "You can't be serious, Sloan?" She looked at the others.

Greta and Christian held each other and Elliott walked over to his parents and stood by them. Greta placed her hand on Elliott's shoulder.

Sloan Moonbeam placed his arm on the hearth of the fireplace and looked at the flame for a few seconds. His pale face reflected the fire's light.

He turned and looked at Syballine and said, "I am serious. It's the best plan that I can come up with. I'll lead it, and I will take all the chances with Noir and his dark magic. All I need from you is an alliance. You all know that the red and black dragons and Noir's warriors will attack Moonstone before crossing over to the non-magical world at midnight."

Greta and Christian agreed. Greta looked at the others and said, "He is right. The villagers are meeting today to form an alliance to fight Noir. They know that Enchantra has been captured. They know about the Halloween Crystal. They figured it all out when Noir captured Enchantra and attacked the Island of Orange and Blue."

Greta looked down. Christian looked at his wife with a concern and spoke up, "There's more, Sloan. They are all unhappy with us—especially you. They are questioning why Enchantra chose us to be the guardians. They've lost faith in her judgement and her leadership because of what happened." Christian's hardened face looked at his friend.

Mr. Moonbeam turned towards the fireplace again. What was it? He was on the verge of something . . . some memory. He knew something was going to happen, but he didn't know what it was . . . Someone will help? He remembered that Enchantra had said that. It was in the clearing in the forest—Wolf's End. And, he knew, but he wasn't the only one who knew.

"Mr. Moonbeam's plan is good. I know it," Elliott said.

Syballine looked at Elliott. "You're just a child Elliott. A boy. You can't possibly know how to win this fight."

Greta held her son tighter. She looked at Syballine and said, "Elliott loves his teacher, Syballine. He just wants things to be okay."

Elliott looked up at his mother, "It's not that mom. It's that I have a feeling. And, that's not all."

Mr. Moonbeam turned towards Elliott. His cape flowed behind him as he walked away from the warm fire and knelt down to make eye contact with his student.

"What else, Elliott?" he asked in a warm, soft tone.

Elliott looked at his teacher and said, "The others . . . I can see them. I see Sabrina and I see Enchantra. They are standing in Noir's castle and I see Noir. He is meeting with his warriors, Odin, and some others . . . vampires, werewolves, and ghosts from the Dark Lands. And, Noir's magic is reaching out. He is sending messages throughout the Dark Lands. They are all gathering right now. The monsters, the vampires, the werewolves . . . they are running through the trees the trees that have an endless, sad song."

Elliott put his arms around Mr. Moonbeam's neck and hugged him. He was shaking. He was scared.

Greta reached down and said, "What's going on, Sloan. Why is Elliott seeing all of this?"

She tried to hold her son, but he would not let go of Mr. Moonbeam.

"It's okay, Elliott. Everything is going to be okay," he stood up with Elliott in his arms and handed Elliott to Christian.

Mr. Moonbeam turned towards Syballine. He walked closer to her and extended his hands. She walked to him and hugged him. Sloan Moonbeam knew that she understood what was happening.

They both turned to look at Elliott and his parents. Christian was still holding his son when Mr. Moonbeam said, "Elliott is a Truth See'er."

Elliott's parents were silent.

Mr. Moonbeam walked towards them and said, "And that's not all. He will have to come with me, into Noir's castle to retrieve the Dark Diamond of

Disappearance. He will have to help us banish Noir from Moonstone."

    Christian squeezed his son tightly.

23

A TOWN MEETING

Mr. Moonbeam and the others walked into the very old Moonstone Village Hall with both confidence and concern. As the day continued, each hour brought them closer and closer to midnight and Mr. Moonbeam new it was time to act before that critical moment when Noir and his evil warriors would be able to crossover into the non-magical world.

All around them, the villagers of Moonstone, who were seated in wooden chairs, spoke in hushed voices. Mr. Moonbeam could see the look of concern on every face, but once the villagers saw him and the others enter the room, the talking stopped. Everyone looked at Mr. Moonbeam.

"This is your fault, Sloan. You are to blame," one villager said.

"Thanks to you we have nothing. Noir's dragons burned our cottage down to ashes," cried a woman.

"You were sent by Enchantra to be a guardian of the non-magical world. You were supposed to protect the crystal and hide its powers from Noir. You failed, Sloan Moonbeam," said another villager.

Despite the insults, Mr. Moonbeam walked proudly by each one of the witches, warlocks, wizards, and magical gypsies that filled the old Moonstone Village Hall. A tall skinny man with a large nose stood at the front of the room.

"Well . . . well . . . look who's here? If it isn't the great guardians of Moonstone." He stood by the podium.

"Hello Sherman," Mr. Moonbeam said.

"Did you come to apologize for the destruction you and the other guardians allowed to happen or did you come to lay out some worthless plan to fix this mess?" Mr. Moonbeam looked hard at his former classmate. He and Sherman had attended wizarding school together and as children never got along. However, Mr. Moonbeam knew that he deserved the hostility and anger directed at him. He could take it. He could handle it.

A TOWN MEETING

The crowd was silent as Mr. Moonbeam said, "Yes. I do have a plan for defeating Noir."

The crowd laughed and some of the witches booed at Mr. Moonbeam. Sherman slammed his gavel down on the podium and stepped aside so that Mr. Moonbeam could speak.

Mr. Moonbeam walked up to the podium. On the outside he appeared calm before the angry crowd. However, on the inside, his mind raced with many doubts and questions. Why had Enchantra selected him to be a guardian? Why did he have to assume all of this responsibility?

He thought back to when he was a young boy and remembered how Enchantra had told his parents that he would be special. But how could he be special? He looked at Elliott. Elliott was special. Elliott, like Enchantra, was a Truth See'er. Elliott came from a long line of important witches and warlocks all of whom were highly skilled and educated. Mr. Moonbeam's parents were just simple villagers. His father made and sold shoes. His mother was a simple housewife who tended a magical herb garden.

He looked at the villagers in front of him. Some of them he had known his whole life. Many of them were also simple farm folk who worked simple jobs and tended to gardens. They farmed crops and raised animals. They built their cottages by hand. They cut the wood themselves and gathered stones to build their fireplaces. How had he managed to rise from being a simple villager to being a guardian stationed in the non-magical world? How did he get to be Noir's adversary? As he looked at the silent crowd and realized his failings, he also began to realize his successes in a way that he had never realized before.

Years of studying witchcraft, magic, teaching and learning had gotten him to this point. And now, the people of Moonstone depended on him. He looked down at Elliott. He knew Elliott was concerned. He looked at Syballine and knew that she longed for her daughter. He looked at Christian and Greta and knew that they were overjoyed with pride knowing that their only son was a Truth See'er, but they were also weary with concern knowing that Elliott's powers would ultimately be used for measures beyond even his control—starting now.

Mr. Moonbeam's quiet voice resonated as he addressed the crowd, "Hello everyone. Today is Halloween and it won't be long before midnight approaches."

The villagers listened as the autumn winds howled outside the old wooden building. It was a cloudy evening.

A TOWN MEETING

Mr. Moonbeam continued, "As the chief guardian of the non-magical world, Enchantra placed great responsibility on me to not only protect our world but to also protect the non-magical world. For non-magical people can never know of our magical world and way of life—it is forbidden—and written down in the Witches' Code of Conduct and those laws were written ages ago by the first witches of Moonstone. But, as you know, Noir was able to use a ghost to gain entrance into the non-magical world, and he was able to use that ghost to place a spell on his own daughter, Sabrina and kidnap her. But even worse, he took the Halloween Crystal, but all of you know this already."

The crowd became restless and murmured amongst themselves. Mr. Moonbeam gave them a chance to talk and when it stopped, he continued.

"We all know why Noir captured the Halloween Crystal. He is evil and greedy and sees himself as a god worthy of ruling over every living thing in Moonstone and the non-magical world. But, I am here to tell you that I will stop him—even if I have to lose my own life."

Elliott, who was sitting in the front row with his parents, felt overwhelmingly sad for his teacher.

"And what exactly is your plan, Sloan Moonbeam? Because before you all showed up, we were in the process of forming our own plan!" Sherman exclaimed.

The crowd murmured again and Mr. Moonbeam waited.

"I've been to the Island of Orange and Blue. I've seen the destruction and death. I buried the orange and blue mermaids myself and stopped the fires with my own magic. Then, I saw the image of Ginny Butler's ghost in the mirror next to Enchantra's throne."

The crowd gasped.

Mr. Moonbeam continued, "Noir lied to her just as he lies to everyone else. Ginny's ghost is angry and wants revenge. She wants to help us defeat Noir. See for yourself." Mr. Moonbeam pointed to the large mirror that hung on the wall behind the podium.

Within seconds, the hazy, white ghost of Ginny Butler appeared, circling the mirror. The crowd gasped in astonishment. Elliott was awestruck.

"You have some nerve, Sloan Moonbeam, sending us the very ghost that helped Noir capture the Halloween Crystal—the same ghost that kidnapped Syballine's daughter," Sherman said.

Syballine stood up from the front row and

A TOWN MEETING

addressed Sherman. "Let him speak Sherman. Sloan knows what he's doing," she said.

Mr. Moonbeam gestured towards the mirror and used his magic to dim the candles in the old room with its white walls and wooden furniture. For throughout the great hall, portraits of old wizards and witches, that hung on the walls, looked back at the crowd as the candlelight faded.

Behind the podium, the mirror turned red, then green, and finally purple as the ghost spoke to the crowd.

"So sad . . . so sad . . . Noir is a liar . . . he lied to me. He promised me my husband. He promised me that we would be reunited. I will tell you . . . that right now . . . he is plotting his conquest. For I know, I can spy through his mirrors. In his dark castle, he is standing on his balcony sending out his magic. He holds the Halloween Crystal and from all over the Dark Lands his minions are gathering . . . the werewolves, the vampires, the hags and monsters are coming. They are headed towards his castle and he is waiting on them. Standing on his balcony, surrounded by his red and black dragons who circle the dark castle. At midnight, he will use the crystal to enter the non-magical world but first he will destroy and rule what is left of this world. He will ruin all of Moonstone . . . so sad . . . so sad . . . so sad." The ghost circled the purplish mirror—a white haze that turned and turned.

"Enough of this. We will form our own alliance without all of this ghostly nonsense," Sherman shouted.

The crowd became restless and Ginny's ghost thrust itself out of the mirror and circled throughout the old village hall and hovered over the crowd. The ghost lunged towards Sherman and scared him. Then, the ghost flew back into the mirror. The hundreds and hundreds of magical candles flickered.

Mr. Moonbeam turned towards the ghost and said, "Enough spooking, Ginny. You will follow my orders now. Do you understand?"

The ghost calmed down and the mirror turned from purple to green and only a calm white haze of Ginny's face remained.

Mr. Moonbeam spoke, "I order you, Ginny Butler. I order you to show them the only way to defeat Noir. Show them in the mirror!" Elliott watched his teacher's face go from humble to serious in seconds as Mr. Moonbeam walked closer to the mirror behind the podium.

The crowd watched as the vision in the mirror showed Noir's gothic castle. The vision went through the castle, through twists and turns and secret passageways and stairways, through checkered floors and rooms with thick wooden furniture and hallways with ghostly portraits of Noir looking like a vampire. The vision took them throughout the dark, damp castle with its candles, rugs, and tapestries, until it finally came to a chamber with a velvet case of glistening jewels situated next to a golden throne with red cushions. Within the case of glistening blue jewels was a single black jewel—enormous in size. Mr. Moonbeam said, "Behold . . . the Dark Diamond of Disappearance!" Everyone gasped.

24

A SECRET WEAPON

EVERYONE WAS IN SHOCK, BUT DEEP down the villagers knew. They knew that they were no match for Noir's magic—especially now that he possessed the Halloween Crystal. The Dark Diamond of Disappearance was one of only a few power sources capable of defeating Noir. It was an equal match of power to the Halloween Crystal and they knew that.

Sherman was the first to speak, "This is dangerous magic, Sloan Moonbeam. Do you know the risks?"

Mr. Moonbeam looked at his old classmate. He knew that Sherman would always try to undermine any idea or act that he should ever try to implement. He wasn't surprised.

Mr. Moonbeam said, "Of course I know the risks of using the Dark Diamond. If I'm not careful, Moonstone could be cast away into total darkness, forever."

The crowd murmured to themselves. Mr. Moonbeam looked behind and watched Ginny's ghost circle in the mirror.

Someone in the crowd spoke up, "So you are willing to carry the Dark Diamond of Disappearance yourself, Sloan Moonbeam? Even Noir himself is afraid to use its dark magic! How can you possibly handle such power?"

Another villager spoke, "And better yet, how do you plan to get to the diamond? Nobody who enters Noir's castle comes out alive."

Mr. Moonbeam looked at the crowd. All eyes were on him. It seemed that no matter what he did or where he turned there was always resistance. Always doubt. But, looking out before him, he knew in his heart and his mind that this was the only way to defeat Noir.

He said, "I will do it. I will enter Noir's lair and with the help of Ginny Butler's ghost, I will find my way to the chamber where Noir keeps his gems and the Dark Diamond."

A SECRET WEAPON

For behind Mr. Moonbeam, Ginny's Butler's ghost circled the mirror repeatedly saying, "So sad . . . so sad . . . revenge . . . revenge."

Sherman looked at the ghost and said, "How can you possibly trust this ghost? She's betrayed all of Moonstone before. She did it centuries ago when she married a mortal man and she did it again when she helped Noir steal the Halloween Crystal and kidnap Sabrina."

The crowd murmured again and became very restless. It was then that Elliott got out of his chair and walked up the wooden stairs to the stage and stood next to his teacher. There was a moment of silence as Elliott looked at Mr. Moonbeam and then he turned to the crowd to say, "I will help Mr. Moonbeam find the Dark Diamond of Disappearance. Together we will defeat Noir."

Elliott could not believe the laughter and ridicule that came from the crowd before him. He watched as villager after villager laughed and mocked him saying, "You're just a boy! How could a boy possibly defeat Noir? You aren't a secret weapon . . . you're just a boy!"

Elliott listened and he felt different. He felt heavier like a new weight had been placed on his shoulders. He clenched his fist as tears filled his eyes. He looked at his teacher. He looked at his parents and Syballine. He felt like he was losing control of his magic when suddenly he couldn't hold it in any longer.

He said, "I will help Mr. Moonbeam. You'll see! You don't know what you're talking about. Because I . . . I . . . I am a Truth See'er!"

Elliott didn't realize it, but in anger, his magic had worked to make his voice heard to all the villagers. They had heard his every word despite their laughing and were forced into silence by Elliott's words and thoughts.

Mr. Moonbeam pulled Elliott closer to him. They both stood in front of the crowd. Elliott looked at his parents. He knew that they were proud of him, but he also knew they were concerned—worried about him—and he didn't really understand why.

Sherman said, "A Truth See'er? Is this true? How do you know, Sloan Moonbeam?"

Mr. Moonbeam said, "We know. All of us." He pointed to Syballine and Elliott's parents.

One villager shouted, "What evidence do you have to show that the boy is a Truth See'er? Only Enchantra can decide whether or not the boy is a Truth See'er."

Mr. Moonbeam walked away from the podium. He said, "Elliott has shown us his powers on several

A SECRET WEAPON

occasions. His visions showed us that Noir had attacked the Island of Orange and Blue. He saw it all in his mind's eye. Elliott's mind led us to uncover the truth about Ginny Butler by leading us to her diary which was kept in an old mansion in the non-magical world. As his teacher in the non-magical world, he has shown me that he has the ability to predict events. But here in Moonstone, his powers are heightened and accurate. He is indeed a Truth See'er. And with Elliott by my side, we will be able to navigate through Noir's castle, using Ginny Bulter's ghost to help us. Ginny will be present in the mirrors of the castle and will point us in the right direction and Elliott will be there to make sure that our pathway is correct."

Elliott felt proud. His anger and fear were now replaced with pride. He felt important. For the first time in his life, he felt like a true witch and he had Mr. Moonbeam to thank for it. He loved Moonstone. He loved being around his own people. Once the fight was over, he would tell his parents that he wanted to stay. In Moonstone, he felt like somebody. He had powers. He was a Truth See'er and he would help the people of Moonstone.

Elliott didn't know it but his thoughts were magically transferred to the crowd before him, his teacher, and his parents in a magical wave of conscious thought. They stared at the young boy standing next to his teacher, and they knew it was true. Elliott had managed to silence the crowd twice. They had perceived his thoughts enter their own minds and only a Truth See'er was capable of such magic. What was once resistance now turned into complete joy and hope. They all cheered! Elliott smiled.

Mr. Moonbeam, although happy for Elliott, felt the weight of the world on his shoulders. He would have to protect Elliott in the castle because Truth See'ers were rare. He would have to hold the Dark Diamond of Disappearance. He would have to make sure the diamond's magic exiled only Noir and did not get out of hand and exile the entire world of Moonstone into total darkness. And, he would have to do all of it before midnight to stop Noir and his villains from entering the non-magical world on Halloween.

Elliott heard his teacher's thoughts. He looked at Mr. Moonbeam and said, "Don't worry Mr. Moonbeam. Everything will be okay."

25

THE BATTLE BEGINS

While it was true that Elliott and Mr. Moonbeam felt secure in their efforts to enter Noir's lair and steal the Dark Diamond of Disappearance, behind every feeling of confidence and commitment, there are also feelings of withdrawal and fear.

For Elliott, the fear was real. He had to face his fear that his magic could fail. For it wasn't too long ago that his unpredictable magic had caused him a myriad of problems in his classroom. But now, there was no time for failure. He had to be there with Mr. Moonbeam and use his ability to see the truth to help Mr. Moonbeam navigate through Noir's castle using Ginny Butler's guidance.

Mr. Moonbeam also struggled with fear. He was afraid of so many things. He was afraid of losing the battle. He feared for the villagers who had to distract Noir and fight for Moonstone. He feared for Elliott having so much responsibility, and he feared for Elliott's parents who were no doubt worried about Elliott entering Noir's castle.

Halloween was here. Mr. Moonbeam stood at the base of the mountains and looked at the looming castle in the darkness. He held Elliott close to his cape. Elliott had never seen such a frightening castle. It was gigantic.

The dark castle towered over the valley of sad trees that surrounded the mountain on which it sat. From far away, Elliott could see that each small window in the castle glowed with a red light which further accentuated the darkness of the gothic castle with its tall steeples, turrets, and towers all connected to form the immense structure. Elliott could see a connecting bridge that led to one tall tower that loomed over the entire castle.

"That's where we will find Noir's lair, Mr. Moonbeam." He pointed to the castle's tower in front of the bright moon.

THE BATTLE BEGINS

"Getting there will be the hard part," Mr. Moonbeam said. He looked around the Dark Lands and felt sad. It was such a sad place. And, the eternal metallic song of the trees made it even sadder. Their leaves chimed like sad bells in the night. The sad song made its way through the dark, gray valley to the mountains above.

Elliott shivered a little. "Mr. Moonbeam, do you remember when we entered Mossy Mansion and you gave me some new magical clothes? Could you do that again?" Elliott asked.

Mr. Moonbeam smiled. Despite the scary and difficult task of entering Noir's lair, being with Elliott always made Mr. Moonbeam feel good. Elliott was able to bring out the "teacher" in Mr. Moonbeam, so he pulled out his wand and waved it in the air. Spinning around and around he said:

By the magic of the moon
And all its might...
Give this young boy the clothes of a witch or a wizard...
Tonight!

And just like before at Mossy Mansion, Elliott was immediately given the same clothes as before—a dark suit with a green vest and a witchy green hat. In his hand he held a black wand with a green tip that glowed in the darkness.

Elliott smiled. He looked at his teacher who hadn't changed his outfit in days.

"What about you?" he asked. "If we are going to do this, we deserve new clothes at least. Don't you think? And, your hair is a mess, Mr. Moonbeam."

Mr. Moonbeam laughed and with one magical gesture of his hand he immediately freshened up his wardrobe with a complete change. He was the old Mr. Moonbeam again with his dark cape, purple vest, and shiny suit. Along with this, he wore his magical, black top hat and white gloves.

In his hand, Mr. Moonbeam carried his black wand. Elliott was happy to see his teacher's shiny, wavy hair neatly in place, under his top hat.

Elliott thought that Mr. Moonbeam looked like the ghost of an old magician as his cape and hair blew in the night. Mr. Moonbeam pulled Snowflake out of his cape and told the bird to fly high to the castle and keep watch from the tower. Elliott watched Snowflake fly towards the castle, but he was immediately startled when Mr. Moonbeam pulled him closer.

Suddenly, the night sky was filled with hundreds of witches on brooms. They were headed towards Noir's castle. Each one had a weapon or magical device in hand for the battle that was going to begin.

In the gray valley below Noir's castle, his vampires, werewolves, and monsters congregated in one large

THE BATTLE BEGINS

mass of evil—their growls and voices could be heard throughout the Dark Lands. From the balcony of his castle, Noir stood and held the Halloween Crystal in his hand. He pointed it towards the moon and a beam of immense power shot out from the crystal towards the night sky. Then, he used the crystal to levitate down towards his dark army.

Noir looked around and saw the witches and wizards circling his castle. He had not predicted this surprise attack.

With Greta, Christian and Syballine leading the attack, the witches of Moonstone swamped Noir's dark army from above riding on their broomsticks. Christian threw several of his red daggers towards the red and black dragons that came charging towards him. Greta used her magic crystal to transform into a blue dragon. Leaving her broom behind, she charged towards the vampires below blowing her own breath of fire and fanning her wings.

Syballine used her own dark magic to create a forcefield that enclosed a large group of werewolves. Meanwhile, Noir continued to charge his minions to fight while holding the Halloween Crystal towards the night sky.

"Now's our time, Elliott," Mr. Moonbeam whispered.

Elliott felt nervous as the two of them walked quickly along the mountainous pathway towards the great black castle with its sinister red windows. Elliott tried not to look at the fight taking place in the valley behind him. Small raindrops started to pelt their faces.

"Mr. Moonbeam . . . it's raining," said Elliott.

Mr. Moonbeam heard Elliott but paid no attention. Time was wasting. He knew that Noir was using the Halloween Crystal to puncture a small hole between Moonstone and the non-magical world and that hole would grow in the sky until the portal was large enough for all of his warriors to enter.

They came to the large drawbridge of the castle and hurried across like two dark spies in the night. Once inside, Elliott took a deep breath and stood in amazement. He had never seen such an elegantly decorated hallway with an arched ceiling, tapestries, and rugs that seemed to go on forever. It was cold in the castle.

Elliott was taken by surprise when Mr. Moonbeam suddenly pulled him into a dark corner and covered his mouth. They stood in silence as Noir's accomplice, Odin, walked by. Odin looked like the devil and Elliott held his breath—afraid to move. They watched

THE BATTLE BEGINS

as Odin walked through the hallway towards the drawbridge.

"Be very quiet, Elliott. We must find a mirror," Mr. Moonbeam said.

They walked down the dark hallway. Elliott looked at all the portraits of Noir's dragons. There were dozens of large portraits on the walls. At the end of the hallway was a huge table with a ghostly candelabra that illuminated the dark passage.

"There's a mirror, Mr. Moonbeam." Elliott pointed to a mirror behind the table.

Mr. Moonbeam clutched the crystal that hung from the necklace around his neck. He felt safe knowing that they could transform into another figure thanks to Greta's transformation crystal if needed. Quietly, they walked towards the mirror.

Mr. Moonbeam spoke, "Ginny Butler . . . Ginny . . . we are in the castle."

Elliott thought Mr. Moonbeam's face looked spooky talking to the mirror by candlelight. They waited for a second and then the white, hazy, ghostly, face of Ginny Butler appeared in the mirror.

"Sloan Moonbeam . . . for it's a checkered hallway you seek. Follow the steps to the left until the checkered floor you meet." The ghost pointed to a set of concrete steps to the left.

Elliott had never seen such sinister looking concrete steps. Mr. Moonbeam grabbed Elliott's hand and started towards the stairs.

"Do you trust Ginny's ghost, Elliott?" Mr. Moonbeam asked.

Elliott cleared his thoughts and focused his mind on his magic. Everything felt right. He had no apprehension.

"Yes, Mr. Moonbeam. I think this is the way," he said.

Mr. Moonbeam nodded. Together they started up the cold dark staircase which turned for each floor of the castle. They came to a hallway with a red floor. On the walls hung spooky portraits of Noir, who looked like a vampire, in various poses.

They continued up the winding stairs to another floor of the castle which was completely black and white. Staring down the long hallway of this floor, Elliott immediately got a bad feeling.

"Mr. Moonbeam . . . we are not alone here," Elliott said. Mirrors hung along the walls of the hallway and the two dark avengers could see ghostly reflections in the mirrors.

THE BATTLE BEGINS

They could hear ghostly cries for help. Mr. Moonbeam covered Elliott's ears and picked him up and headed for the next floor.

They stood motionless and took a few minutes to catch their breath when Elliott opened his eyes and looked at the vast hallway that stretched before him. It was a checkered floor, just like Ginny's ghost had said. The green and black checkered floor extended to the end of a long hallway. At the end of the hallway there was a large wooden table with candles situated on either side of what appeared to be some kind of altar. There was a mirror on the wall behind the table. There were two arched stone doorways to the left and right of the large wooden table.

Mr. Moonbeam held Elliott's hand as the two walked slowly down the checkered hallway towards the mirror.

Elliott could hear the sound of water dripping. He could hear the battle outside.

Waiting for them at the end of the hallway was Ginny Butler's ghost in the mirror.

The ghost spoke, "Sloan Moonbeam... congratulations. You're almost there..."

26

SEPARATION

Mr. Moonbeam looked intently at the ghost in the mirror. For never before had there been a Halloween like this one . . .

"Sloan Moonbeam . . . you must separate," the ghost said.

Elliott felt nervous but brave at the same time. Separate? What was this crazy ghost talking about?

"No time for games, Ginny Butler. Time is running out. You must lead us to the Dark Diamond. Now, tell me where it is," Mr. Moonbeam pleaded.

Elliott noticed that Mr. Moonbeam had changed. His demands now turned into pleas for help from a tormented ghost. Elliott didn't understand.

"Yes, Sloan Moonbeam. Time is running out. For at this very minute Noir is outside with the Halloween Crystal opening the veil between the two worlds." The ghostly face in the mirror disappeared and Mr. Moonbeam and Elliott looked hard at the scene shown in the mirror. It was the battle outside, and Elliott could see Noir holding the crystal in the air. A ray of power split through the night sky, like a beam of lightning, opening a portal into the non-magical world.

With each second, the portal grew larger and larger, illuminated by the moon but not covered by the clouds.

The image shifted to the ground and Elliott could see his parents and the others fighting the vampires, werewolves, and demons while the trees played their sad metallic song.

He watched his father throw his glowing daggers at several dragons. He watched the witches and wizards on broomsticks fight to keep the dark forces down. He watched several witches fall through the night sky. All of them hit with magic from the forces below.

Mr. Moonbeam spoke urgently, "Tell us Ginny. Tell us what to do. And you know, you know that

SEPARATION

I will keep my promise. Once I get the Halloween Crystal from Noir, I will return to Mossy Mansion, and I will find the spirit of your long-lost husband. You will be reunited. I promise you that. You have my word," Mr. Moonbeam said.

The ghost circled the mirror, "Noir made the same promise to Ginny . . . so sad . . . so sad."

Mr. Moonbeam grew nervous. "Yes, but Noir is a liar. He cheated you out of a bargain. You have my word. I will not lie to you, Ginny Butler. I will not lie."

Elliott watched wide-eyed as the ghost looked at him.

The ghost spoke in a raspy voice, "The boy . . . the boy knows all truths. Tell me boy . . . is your teacher telling the truth?"

Elliott's palms were sweaty. He held his wand in his hand. What good did it do? He couldn't force Ginny Butler to tell them which way to go. He couldn't magically stop the battle outside. What could he do? He looked at his teacher. Mr. Moonbeam was nervous. Mr. Moonbeam was anxious.

But, Elliott could sense what he had always known. Mr. Moonbeam was a good man. When Mr. Moonbeam made a promise, he meant it. He knew that Mr. Moonbeam would indeed risk his own life to reunite Ginny with the spirit of her husband. Elliott knew that Mr. Moonbeam would risk his own life to save both worlds from Noir. Elliott knew that Mr. Moonbeam's word was as good as gold.

He looked at the ghost and said, "You can trust him. Mr. Moonbeam is a good man." Elliott felt proud saying that. He was no longer afraid of Ginny's ghost.

Ginny's ghost took a deep raspy breath and said, "Good. Sloan Moonbeam . . . if you lie to me I will haunt you down for the rest of your life. And the boy too! You will never know peace."

Mr. Moonbeam looked at the ghost and said, "I understand."

The ghost drew back and pointed in both directions with her ghostly white hands which trailed like a haze of smoke from the crystal, clear mirror.

The ghost said, "To the left, you'll find the bridge to the tower and the Dark Diamond. To the right, you'll find the girl."

"Sabrina?" Elliott asked.

"Yes . . . Sabrina . . . so sad . . . so sad . . ." Ginny spoke. "Make your choice, Sloan Moonbeam. Make your choice. But know that you will not forget Ginny Butler. My ghost will find you." Ginny disappeared, but Elliott knew she'd return.

SEPARATION

Mr. Moonbeam and Elliott stood on the checkered floor by the mirror and looked at the two spooky concrete, arched doorways on either side of them.

"I'll go after Sabrina," Elliott said. "Then, I'll take her out of the castle. You . . . you must go after the diamond and then you must go after Noir. I believe in you, Mr. Moonbeam."

"But it's dangerous for you to go alone, Elliott," Mr. Moonbeam said remembering how he had left Sabrina alone in Mossy Mansion.

He reached inside his pocket and took out Storm. The miniature horse grew before Elliott's eyes—illuminating the darkness of the room. Then, without warning Snowflake flew in from the doorway to the left—further affirming the direction to the tower's bridge. The bird perched itself on Elliott's shoulder and Mr. Moonbeam used his magic to levitate Elliott onto Storm's back.

But, Elliott said nothing. He simply looked at his teacher and smiled. Despite the dark spookiness around them, this was the best Halloween adventure he had ever had. He knew he would be okay. His powers told him that. And Mr. Moonbeam had given him Storm and Snowflake for protection and company. He was not alone.

Sitting on the glowing horse, Elliott said, "Everything will be okay, Mr. Moonbeam. You go and defeat Noir. Go save Halloween. We will rescue Sabrina, and I will be there when you need me."

A single tear fell down Mr. Moonbeam's cheek as he left Elliott, Storm, and Snowflake, and headed through the dark, arched doorway.

27

THE DARK DIAMOND OF DISAPPEARANCE

MR. MOONBEAM BOLTED UP THE DARK stairwell to the high bridge which connected the main part of the castle to the tower that loomed over everything. Faster and faster he ran across the bridge. Mr. Moonbeam's cape flapped in the wind as he ran. Looking up into the night sky, he felt the moon's energy add more power to his already determined resolve. So far, his plan was working. The portal to the non-magical world was growing. Time was running out.

Bolting through the door, Mr. Moonbeam burst into Noir's lair and was taken by surprise when he found Odin, Noir's right-hand man, standing in front of Noir's throne.

"Well, Sloan Moonbeam. Noir was wondering where you were?" Odin said sarcastically.

Mr. Moonbeam stood in a strong stance with his fists clenched and stared at the villain.

"Get out of my way, devil," Mr. Moonbeam declared.

"Noir is opening the portal right at this minute. Already his ghosts, vampires, and werewolves are beginning their levitation into the sky towards the portal. You have only a few minutes until midnight. But, Noir knew that you were not in the battle—for whatever reason—he left me behind to guard his power sources." Odin and Mr. Moonbeam circled one another in a standoff.

"Is that why you're here?" he asked.

"It doesn't matter why I'm here. Get out of my way." And with those words Mr. Moonbeam pointed his wand at the evil wizard. A beam of magic whizzed from the tip of his wand and knocked Odin to the ground. But Odin immediately got up. He lunged at Mr. Moonbeam bearing his sharp teeth.

THE DARK DIAMOND OF DISAPPEARANCE

Mr. Moonbeam wrestled the villain onto the floor. They fought—twisting and turning—knocking over tables, books, and mirrors. Yes, there were mirrors everywhere. As he wrestled Odin, Mr. Moonbeam saw the ghostly face of Ginny Butler in one of the mirrors. She watched Mr. Moonbeam struggle to restrain Odin. Could she help? What could she do?

All around him, the beautiful mirrors that decorated Noir's dark lair began to shatter and burst. Glass was scattered all over the floor. Odin looked up, distracted by the broken mirrors and Mr. Moonbeam was able to throw a punch which knocked Odin on his back.

Mr. Moonbeam watched as dozens of ghostly figures emerged from the broken mirrors. The ghosts encircled Odin who was lying on the floor. In terror, he looked at the ghostly figures all around him. Mr. Moonbeam covered his face with his cape and stood back in a corner. He listened to the screams but didn't dare watch as these tormented spirits—no longer held captive in Noir's magical mirrors—carried Odin through the open door to the ghostly battle outside.

Mr. Moonbeam waited until it was quiet. Then, he uncovered his face and looked at the destroyed room. However, the mirror behind Noir's throne was not broken. In that mirror, Mr. Moonbeam looked at the ghostly face of Ginny Butler.

Ginny's face was different now. She smiled at him and said, "There Sloan Moonbeam. There is the case of jewels. Take the Dark Diamond and go . . . go before it's too late."

Mr. Moonbeam moved through the clutter and debris towards the velvet case that held a variety of black and blue gems. They all glistened in the darkness and he knew that the large black one was indeed the Dark Diamond of Disappearance. He held the glowing diamond in his hand and stared at it for a minute before the image in the mirror caught his attention.

In the mirror, he saw Elliot, Sabrina, Snowflake, and Storm. They were headed out of the castle towards the mountains. They were safe. Elliott had broken Noir's spell and had rescued Sabrina.

Clutching the black diamond, Mr. Moonbeam looked at the mirror and said, "Thank you, Ginny Butler."

Then he pulled his broom out of his cape and headed towards the doorway. He hopped on his broom and whizzed over the bridge and the castle towards the battle.

28

THE WITCHING HOUR

MR. MOONBEAM FLEW TOWARDS THE battle ahead. The wind hit his face as he pushed his broom to go faster. The excitement of the battle was almost too much for him, but he had to see it through to the end.

Ahead of him, he watched as his fellow witches, wizards, and warlocks used magic to try and hold back Noir's evil forces. But it was clearly too much and the ranks of the good fighters thinned right before his eyes. Greta, Christian, and Syballine were still fighting though, and Mr. Moonbeam watched as they used magic against Noir's monsters.

High above the ground, Noir sat on the back of his mightiest dragon. Suspended in mid-air, with the moon shining behind him, the villain held the Halloween Crystal towards the night sky, opening the portal to the non-magical world.

Mr. Moonbeam watched the portal continue to grow larger. What started out as a small circle widened with each passing second that Noir pointed the great crystal, and its beam of magic, towards the opening.

All around this horrific scene, Mr. Moonbeam flew throughout the vampires, werewolves, and evil magical beasts that were being lifted towards the portal.

It was now close to midnight, and Mr. Moonbeam had to act fast. While he whizzed, twisted, and turned through the floating monsters, he knocked some of them back to the ground with his broom. He pointed his magic wand at some of the monsters and his magical beams of energy sent them plunging towards the ground.

Greta, Christian, and Syballine joined him and together they worked to try and stop the evil magic all around them. But Mr. Moonbeam and his friends knew that there were too many monsters floating towards the portal. They needed to stop the central problem.

THE WITCHING HOUR

The wind blew through Mr. Moonbeam's hair as he shouted, "Try and hold them off from entering the portal. I'm going after Noir!"

The others heard his demand and immediately disbanded. Greta, who was transformed into a blue dragon, used her magic to hold back the red and black dragons. Christian threw his magical daggers every possible way. From his broom, he watched as his magical daggers sent several dragons to the valley below.

Syballine used her night magic to create a force field that blocked many of the evil beings from levitating towards the growing portal in the night sky.

Noir looked down from his dragon and saw Syballine working her magic. He immediately shot rays of magic from his eyes. The rays hit Syballine and knocked her off her broom. She plunged towards the hundreds of screaming vampires on the ground.

From beyond the battlefield, Elliott and Sabrina watched in horror as Syballine tumbled towards the ground. Mr. Moonbeam watched, too. Suddenly, something happened in Elliott's mind that he could not explain. His magic took over, and he imagined in his mind that Syballine was suspended in mid-air—stopped just short from hitting the ground below.

Syballine watched as hundreds of angry vampires hissed at her, but she was safe. What had happened? She was suspended in mid-air and then suddenly Greta flew down and she landed on the back of the blue dragon. She was safe.

Sabrina looked at Elliott. "What happened?" she asked.

Elliott said, "I think my magic saved your mom. I can help them from here. I need to concentrate and see what I can do."

Sabrina pointed towards a white witch who was in a cage on the ground. In the middle of this battle, there was a glowing cage covered by a bright magical spell. It was Enchantra.

Elliott knew that he needed to help rescue Enchantra. But how?

Meanwhile, Mr. Moonbeam focused his attention on Noir. He whizzed even faster towards the evil sorcerer, dodging the levitating villains that floated before him. He stopped in front of Noir—suspended on his broom—and pointed his wand at Noir. He sent out a wave of moon magic that sent a shock through Noir and almost knocked him off his dragon. But Noir held the Halloween Crystal above his head and did not drop it. He pointed its bright magical rays towards the portal in the night sky.

"You think you can stop me, Sloan Moonbeam? I am all powerful!" Noir said.

He pointed his hand towards Mr. Moonbeam and sent a ray of magic towards Mr. Moonbeam while still holding the crystal in his other hand. The crystal's magic continued to levitate the villains towards the hole in the night sky.

Noir's scaly dragon growled at Mr. Moonbeam and Mr. Moonbeam could feel the heat from its fiery breath as he circled his foe. His friends were doing a good job keeping the monsters from rising towards the portal, but Mr. Moonbeam knew that midnight was quickly approaching.

Mr. Moonbeam kept the Dark Diamond in his pocket. When should he use it? He had to knock the Halloween Crystal out of Noir's hand before using the diamond or the Halloween Crystal could disappear into total darkness with Noir—forever.

Like a swift cowboy riding his horse over a vast mountain, Mr. Moonbeam zoomed and circled through the night sky trying his best to knock Noir off of his dragon. He tried to distract Noir from pointing his magic towards the night sky. He got so close that the Halloween Crystal was almost in his hand when

Noir's dragon turned its huge head towards him and sent out a ball of fire that almost sent Mr. Moonbeam tumbling towards the ground.

At that moment, Elliott watched Mr. Moonbeam struggle to win the battle. He had to help. He used his mind to levitate Enchantra's cage high into the air. Enchantra watched in amazement as her cage lifted above the monsters and magically levitated towards the dark mountain path where Elliott and Sabrina watched the battle. Elliott stood wide-eyed and watched as his magic lowered the cage to the ground and the force field that covered the cage disappeared.

Enchantra smiled at the children. Sabrina couldn't believe her eyes.

Elliott looked at Sabrina and said, "Use your fire magic to melt the lock."

Sabrina shook her head in agreement and pointed her purple tipped wand at the huge lock that dangled on the cage and melted it. Enchantra walked out of the cage and stood before the children.

"I knew you would help, Elliott. You are Moonstone's new Truth See'er. This is wonderful news!" she said.

Elliott didn't know what to think.

Meanwhile, Mr. Moonbeam continued his struggle. But, no matter what he did, he could not get the

Halloween Crystal out of Noir's hand. There was less than a minute left until midnight—the Witching Hour—and that meant that the portal would be large enough for Noir and his evil minions to exit Moonstone and travel to the non-magical world.

Mr. Moonbeam took the Dark Diamond out of his pocket. Suspended in mid-air, he held it towards Noir.

Enchantra could see Mr. Moonbeam point the Dark Diamond of Disappearance towards Noir.

Enchantra looked towards Elliott, "You must help your teacher get the Halloween Crystal out of Noir's hand. There's only seconds left."

Elliott knew this already. But what should he do? He had to concentrate. He had to think. He watched the battle before him—everyone did.

Everything seemed to move in slow motion. Elliott watched as Mr. Moonbeam held the Dark Diamond towards Noir. He watched Noir laugh at Mr. Moonbeam—not afraid of the diamond's magic. Noir was too consumed by the power in his hand to think about anything but power, destruction, and winning.

But Elliott closed his mind and everything was calm. In his mind, he imagined the Halloween Crystal floating out of Noir's hands. He imagined its power shifting from Noir to Mr. Moonbeam. And, this actually happened. Noir watched in surprise as the powerful crystal ball moved from his hand, through the night sky, towards Sloan Moonbeam.

Still, the all-powerful veins of magical lighting extended from the crystal towards the portal in the night sky.

Seconds remained as Mr. Moonbeam, who was suspended on his broom, held the Halloween Crystal in one hand and the Dark Diamond in the other. Each enchanted object, a huge force of power in this magical world, was too much power for one man to hold.

Mr. Moonbeam felt the magic overtake his body, his mind, and his soul. He was suddenly overwhelmed with an intense feeling of goodness. He had to do the right thing. A flood of memories flashed before his eyes. He thought of his childhood. He could see his parents and that first meeting so long ago, with Enchantra.

He was in his classroom putting up his Halloween decorations for his students when suddenly he could see Noir's face. Sitting on the back of the red and black dragon, Noir looked at Sloan Moonbeam with shock as one by one the villains below retreated. His vampires, werewolves, and monsters ran through the trees—back to the dark forest of the Dark Lands—defeated.

Sloan Moonbeam held the two mystical power sources in his hand. Like a dream, he watched as the portal to the non-magical world closed up.

Then, right at midnight, he felt his moon magic more powerful than ever. For it was said that when the clock struck the witching hour, a witch's magic grew ten-fold. Now add to that, the fact that he held two extremely powerful magical objects in his hand. What was he to do?

He could see everything below him. He could see his friends staring at him as the autumn winds of the Dark Lands blew wildly. He could see Elliott and Sabrina. He could see Snowflake, Storm, and Enchantra. Mr. Moonbeam's friends and his beloved pets watched as he pointed the Dark Diamond of Disappearance towards Noir.

"No!" Noir shouted as an immense dark magic enveloped both him and Mr. Moonbeam. But Mr. Moonbeam held the Halloween Crystal tightly in his other hand. He gripped the Dark Diamond. He watched everything fade around him. He felt the power overtake all the evil Noir had created—like an erased chalkboard—it was gone.

He thought of his classroom and the cursive letters he had written on the board and how Elliott had struggled to write his letters. Just as he had erased those letters on that first day, the Dark Diamond had erased Noir and his evil.

But Noir wasn't the only one gone. Mr. Moonbeam was gone too. And Elliott and the others looked into the night sky as Sloan Moonbeam and Noir disappeared before their very eyes.

All was silent as Elliott yelled, "Mr. Moonbeam!" And, Elliott's cry for his teacher echoed throughout the Dark Lands...

29

HALLOWEEN

HALLOWEEN IS A MAGICAL TIME OF year, not just in Moonstone, but in the non-magical world as well. On the night that Mr. Moonbeam saved the non-magical world and Moonstone from Noir's destruction, millions of kids around the world dressed in costumes and walked from house to house, saying "trick-or-treat," and bags filled with candies sat on kitchen tables all over the world.

But there's more to Halloween than just trick-or-treating, costumes, and candies. There's tradition—like the tradition of carving a jack-o-lantern with your parents. Or, perhaps you enjoy watching a scary movie with one of your friends each year. Whatever your tradition, Halloween is a magical time of the year.

Mr. Moonbeam had decorated his classroom for his students because he loved Halloween. Mr. Moonbeam had decorated his classroom windows, his classroom closets, the door, and his chalkboard because he wanted his students to appreciate and experience the magic and joy of the season. He had placed a small plastic jack-o-lantern, each one carrying a tiny Halloween eraser, on every desk in his classroom. He wanted to make learning fun. He wanted to show each student that he cared about them.

But that was in the town of Wolf's End, or the town where Mr. Moonbeam and the others had been sent to live with non-magical people and protect their world from Noir and his evil villains. And, Mr. Moonbeam and his friends had fulfilled their task. They had completed their work at the stroke of midnight on Halloween. The little river town called Wolf's End was safe from Noir's evil magic.

But, Elliott felt sad and empty. It was over. The battle was won. And now, he and the others were sitting in the audience of a huge ceremony. For all of Moonstone was now at peace.

HALLOWEEN

The sun was shining, and it was a glorious fall day throughout Moonstone. The orange, red, yellow, and gold leaves of the trees blew in the autumn wind as all the wizards, witches, gypsies, and warlocks of Moonstone sat outside on folding chairs to watch the magical ceremony that Enchantra had requested. Elliott, Sabrina, and their parents were seated on the wooden stage in front of the audience.

Enchantra, dressed in fall colors, stood at the podium and said, "Citizens of Moonstone. It is with a heavy heart that we gather today to celebrate the success of these brave guardians who risked their lives and the lives of their children to save not only our magical world but the non-magical world that we have been blessed to protect."

There was silence. Elliott couldn't understand his feelings. He looked around at the beautiful countryside. He looked at all the magical beings in front of him and wondered . . . Would life ever be the same? How could he go back to the non-magical town of Wolf's End after this experience? His heart was heavy and his mind wandered.

Enchantra continued, "But the main reason we are here is to celebrate and acknowledge the brave contributions of the supreme guardian—the most honorable, brave, and dedicated guardian, teacher, and friend, that I have ever known—Sloan Moonbeam."

The crowd was silent. Nobody said a word.

"Sloan Moonbeam risked his life to save both worlds in a way that had never been done. We will always be grateful for his work. And for his ability to see the truth in the darkest situation . . . " At this moment, Enchantra looked at Elliott and motioned for him to step up to the podium.

"My fellow Moonstonians, meet our youngest, newest Truth See'er, Elliott Keene." The crowd cheered and clapped.

Enchantra continued, "We have Sloan Moonbeam to thank for it. Just like any great teacher should recognize the individual talents of each student, he was able to see Elliott's ability and he helped Elliott recognize and use his magical talents. And because of it, we are all safe and Noir is gone. And we will always be grateful."

The crowd cheered as Enchantra stood behind Elliott and placed her hands, on Elliott's shoulders. He was speechless. He didn't deserve this credit. Mr. Moonbeam deserved it! But where was Mr. Moonbeam? Was he truly gone? Elliott concentrated, but he felt like his magical powers were exhausted.

HALLOWEEN

"And now, per your request, since we did not have a proper Halloween this year, we will celebrate tonight. We will light our jack-o-lanterns and bonfires! We will decorate our cottages and houses! We will eat pumpkin spiced cakes and drink apple cider and wear our favorite costumes and celebrate the most magical night of the year!"

The crowd cheered and everyone clapped. Then Enchantra said, "And we will celebrate the life and magic of Sloan Moonbeam. Wherever he is . . . " She pointed to the vast autumn countryside of Moonstone, towards the cornfields and the scarecrows that danced in the wind. She pointed towards the cottages and the autumn mountains and crystal lakes that extended to the ocean—and the beautiful Island of Orange and Blue and the mermaids that protected her castle. As if by magic, all was well again.

30

MAY IT BE

WHILE THE VILLAGERS OF MOONSTONE prepared for a Halloween celebration, things were different at Wolf's End. The tiny little town was quiet on this rainy autumn day. The children watched Saturday morning cartoons and ate their Halloween candy (way too early in the morning for their parents' approval).

The river ran quietly through the town like a giant snake traveling through the autumn trees that covered the mountains. And once again, the smoky haze of warm fires floated from the chimneys and all was quiet as it was in Moonstone.

And the dilapidated old mansion that sat on Rose Hill stood tall. It stared down through the rain, the mist, and the smoky hazes, at the quiet, river town. Covered in vines and moss, this was once the great home of Ginny Butler and the general and despite all the years, it still stood tall and proud.

And inside this old mansion, that no mortal dared to enter, hung the portraits of Ginny and her husband—untouched for 200 years. The moth-eaten antique furniture was still there along with the tattered carpet. Everything stood as a reminder of a different time.

On the antique table that stood next to the couch, the same old lantern that Elliott and Sabrina had lit together with Mr. Moonbeam was still there. And, for some reason, Elliott who was still in Moonstone, could see these visions while the others decorated for the Halloween party. He walked to a quiet place by some trees and let these visions take over his mind. And for a few moments, he forgot all about Moonstone's Halloween party.

The vision took him back to Mossy Mansion and the vision went past the old portrait of Ginny and the general. It went past the old velvet couch and the antique lamps. It went past the old vacant fireplace to the dilapidated staircase that led to the rooms above. Elliott remembered and a lump formed in his throat as he held back tears.

He and Mr. Moonbeam had found Ginny Butler's diary in the old library and the vision took him past that old library towards the room at the end of the hallway. This was the room that Sabrina had entered—the room where Ginny Butler had placed a spell on her.

Elliott watched the vision get closer and closer to that doorway. His heart beat faster. What was it? He wiped a tear from his face.

The vision moved closer and closer towards the old wooden door. The door opened and inside the dark room stood the old purple moth-eaten canopy bed. Elliott's heart beat faster. Elliott saw Mr. Moonbeam. He was standing next to the bed and he was holding the Halloween Crystal and its magic brightened the dark room.

Elliott felt as if his heart could jump out of his chest. Mr. Moonbeam was alive! He was at Mossy Mansion!

He brushed away the tears and swallowed the lump in his throat. He looked at the others, who were decorating for the party, and he wanted to scream. He wanted to shout, "Mr. Moonbeam's alive! He's alive." But, he couldn't.

He could tell that Mr. Moonbeam was tired. He could tell that he had not rested. Elliott watched the vision continue.

Mr. Moonbeam walked towards the wardrobe closet and slowly opened the doors. Inside the closet was the oval mirror. It looked new even though Elliott knew it had been in the closet for about 200 years.

Elliott looked closely. He saw Ginny Butler's ghost in the mirror.

He watched Mr. Moonbeam hold the Halloween Crystal towards the mirror. Its magic lit up the purple room and Mr. Moonbeam spoke:

May it be...
May it be for Ginny Butler and her husband...
May it be...
Oh, great Halloween Crystal
Search far and wide
Throughout the spirit world...
Find Ginny's husband
And make it right
For a promise I must fulfill...
Before I can rest tonight...

Elliott watched in suspense. His mind's eye told him everything and he felt as if he was there himself. He watched Ginny Butler's ghost move in circles around the oval mirror. The ghost was excited.

Within seconds there was not one ghost but now two. Ginny's husband had joined her and Mr. Moonbeam smiled as he held the crystal and stood in front of the mirror. Mr. Moonbeam's dark hair fell down around his forehead. He looked like the ghost of an old magician in that purplish, lavender room . . . that was so old.

Elliott was stunned as that which was old became new again. The rotted wood of the closet changed. The tattered old canopy became new again. And Mr. Moonbeam also turned around, with the Halloween Crystal in his hand, and watched the magical transformation all around him.

The vision took Elliott through the mansion, which was no longer old and decayed, but new again! It was just as it had been 200 years ago when Ginny and the general had been married! The magical herb garden returned along with the beautiful rejuvenated rose bushes that lined the hill and pathway that surrounded the mansion. Even the old well that stood outside was new again.

Elliott watched as Mr. Moonbeam held the crystal up to the mirror in the wardrobe closet and smiled at Ginny Butler and her husband.

"Congratulations to you both," he said.

Ginny's ghost looked at him and said, "Thank you . . . thank you . . . Sloan Moonbeam."

Mr. Moobeam nodded and said, "You're welcome.

Will I see you again?" he asked as the two ghosts turned away, hand-in-hand.

Ginny turned around and smiled. "Sure you will. After all, we are friends, aren't we?"

Mr. Moonbeam laughed and watched as the two ghosts disappeared beyond the mirror to the realm of the spirit world—together again.

He sighed and closed the two doors of the closet. He felt happy. He felt good.

But, he also felt exhausted. He turned towards the canopy bed. Beside the bed there was an old nightstand. He opened the drawer and carefully placed the Halloween Crystal in the drawer and shut it. Then, he got in bed, closed his eyes, and fell into a deep sleep . . .

31

ONE MORE TIME

Elliott didn't know what to say! He only knew how to feel! He had never felt happier in his life! Mr. Moonbeam was alive and he was resting at Mossy Mansion. He immediately jumped up from his hiding place and ran towards the others.

The villagers of Moonstone had decorated the village hall and the surrounding area for the Halloween party. Elliott looked at all the decorations and smiled to himself. He couldn't believe it. It was going to be a great party. There were hundreds of lit jack-o-lanterns all around him and the wooden tables were filled with food for the party.

He found Sabrina and said, "Mr. Moonbeam is alive! He's alive!"

Sabrina couldn't believe it. "How do you know?" she asked.

"I saw it all. I saw it all in a vision. And he's not just alive, he's asleep at Mossy Mansion. He's super tired and he reunited Ginny Butler with her husband and Mossy Mansion is now new again . . . and."

Elliott's parents walked towards them, "Whoa Elliott . . . calm down. What's this about?" his dad asked. He could tell that Elliott was excited.

Elliott explained to his parents that Mr. Moonbeam was alive and well. He explained each and every detail of his vision and little by little Elliott's excitement got the attention of the others. Syballine, Enchantra, and the other villagers gathered around him and listened to Elliott's account of his vision.

When Elliott was done, everyone turned towards Enchantra. They were speechless.

Enchantra smiled and said, "If Elliott says he's alive. Then, he's alive!"

And there was a thunderous cheer among everybody as the news of Mr. Moonbeam's survival spread throughout all of Moonstone. Everyone was happy.

ONE MORE TIME

And they celebrated by eating candied apples and pumpkin spice muffins. They all put on their Halloween costumes and drank apple cider. They would celebrate Halloween one more time tonight.

They had missed Halloween, but nothing would stop this celebration—even if it wasn't on the thirty-first. They all danced and smiled as the traveling circus musicians played their music. They enjoyed the company of family and friends and everyone was happy knowing that Mr. Moonbeam was alive and well and he was safe.

Elliott danced to the Halloween circus music. He looked at the bonfires and the illuminated jack-o-lanterns. He looked at all the wonderful homemade costumes the villagers had created. He watched all the children eating their candied apples and cookies.

He smiled at Sabrina and looked all around him. The air was crisp with the smell of autumn leaves. Moonstone was a beautiful place and Halloween was here!

And, Mr. Moonbeam would be at school on Monday. He couldn't wait to go to school and see his favorite teacher.

ABOUT THE AUTHOR & ILLUSTRATOR

RYAN COWAN GREW UP IN A SMALL town called Middleport, Ohio. He currently lives in Hawthorne, CA. As a teacher with 20 years of experience, Ryan has taught all grades from K-6th. He currently works as an assistant principal in Los Angeles.

Ryan has degrees and/or credentials in education from the following universities: Marshall University (BFA Music Theory), UCLA (EdM Urban Education), California State University Los Angeles (Multiple Subject Teaching Credential), and California State University Dominguez Hills (Administrative Services Credential).

HALO RIFE IS A FIFTEEN-YEAR-OLD ARTist and illustrator. This is her first time illustrating a children's book. She accredits her artistic talent to her family and friends, who support her endlessly, and to God.

Made in the USA
Monee, IL
17 September 2024

f5a0de13-c27d-430e-a085-d0496771850dR01